Educating
All Students
Together

We would like to dedicate this book to children in our lives who continue to surprise and delight us: Elizabeth Sheehan Opie, Jotham Murray Burrello, Erin Elizabeth Lashley, Alexandra Bethany Beatty Kilgore, and our newest member, Lindsay Sheehan Opie.

Educating All Students Together

How School Leaders Create Unified Systems

LEONARD C. BURRELLO
CARL LASHLEY
EDITH E. BEATTY

CORWIN PRESS, INC.
A Sage Publications Company
Thousand Oaks, California

For information:

Corwin Press, Inc.
A Sage Publications Company
2455 Teller Road
Thousand Oaks, California 91320
E-mail: order@corwinpress.com

Sage Publications Ltd.
6 Bonhill Street
London EC2A 4PU
United Kingdom

Sage Publications India Pvt. Ltd.
M-32 Market
Greater Kailash I
New Delhi 110 048 India

Printed in the United States of America

Library of Congress Cataloging-in-Publication Data

Burrello, Leonard C., 1942-
    Educating all students together: How school leaders create
unified systems / by Leonard C. Burrello, Carl Lashley, Edith E. Beatty.
        p. cm.
    Includes bibliographical references and index.
    ISBN 0-7619-7697-3 (cloth: alk. paper)
    ISBN 0-7619-7698-1 (pbk.: alk. paper)
    1. Inclusive education—United States.   2. Special education—United
States.   3. School management and organization—United States.
4. Education—United States—Evaluation.   I. Lashley, Carl.   II. Beatty
Edith Else, 1951- III. Title.
LC1201.B87 2000
371.9'0973—dc21   00-008747

This book is printed on acid-free paper.

01 02 03 04 05 06 07 7 6 5 4 3 2 1

Corwin Editorial Assistant: Kylee Liegl
Production Editor: Nevair Kabakian
Editorial Assistant: Victoria Cheng
Typesetter/Designer: Tina Hill

Contents

Preface

The public schools work for about 60% of our students. In some schools, the impact of poverty on the family or the family's and community's capacities to value education raises or lowers the number of students who are well served. For selected groups of students, schools do not work well at all. Some of these groups include (a) students who come to school oppressed by the effects of poverty, (b) students who lack parental support, (c) students who are bored, (d) students who come to school with disabilities, (e) students from whom little is expected because of their race, class, or ethnicity, and (f) students for whom school is simply uninteresting. If schools' only purpose were to ensure that all students were academically proficient, the schools would be declared abject failures.

The purpose of the public schools is to create a public (Postman, 1995). Much of that public, however, did not relate to one another before they began school and ceased to relate to each other immediately after high school. It is widely proclaimed that school is the socializing agent that creates the informed citizenry that preserves our democracy and community well being. But schools are also failing at this important social task.

Although school does not work academically or socially, it may not work for other reasons, too. Teaching and learning are not routine, yet the curriculum and instructional processes used in schools emphasize uniformity, regularity, order, and control (Darling-Hammond, 1993). The professional bureaucracy of the public schools does not thrive on difference; it strives for uniformity and standardization. The problem of introducing innovation into schools is primarily an issue of the lack of demand for ideas (Elmore, 1996). Teachers continue to be socialized into the professional bureaucracy, which thwarts their creative instincts to try different approaches for unsuccessful students.

The professional bureaucracy is geared toward the tight coupling of its curriculum to meet state standards. In most school districts the mantra is "Keep the bad guys off our back and raise the test scores." Attempts to change curriculum and instructional practice at the classroom level are more loosely coupled and less subject to administrator direction and control. The loosely coupled nature of organizations—schools specifically—provides practitioners a degree of insulation and cover (Weick, 1976). This tight/loose coupling phenomenon ensures that schools are slow to innovate, even when large numbers of students are not successful at learning.

If we premise schooling on the individual differences students bring to school and use our knowledge of cognition and learning theory to teach valued outcomes, we should be able to create more high performing learning settings for all students. We cannot continue to judge student potential by intelligence or achievement test scores. We must build on every child's inherent curiosity and interest in understanding their world. We need to revisit the definition of student success and engage our communities in a deliberative, democratic planning process to determine how we will acknowledge and value new measures of student learning.

This book is about the moral imperative to nurture students by capitalizing on how they see the world, what their interests are, and how they learn. Schools must acknowledge the variability in students, teachers, schools, and communities and schools to celebrate and capitalize on diversity and complexity. Unleashing the potential of teachers and school site leaders to transform themselves into inquirers who search for and construct meaning for their lives and those of their students is key to our future. We hope the concepts and principles we introduce here help leaders at the school site and in the central office grow with teachers and students and reshape schools so that they become successful and influential in society's minds and lives.

Acknowledgments

The authors would like to acknowledge the work of school leaders and their districts throughout the country whom we have had the pleasure to serve and from whom we have learned so much. We agree with Meg Wheatley that authors create the white space for the voices of practitioners, who already know much of what we have written.

Corwin Press would like to acknowledge the following reviewers:

Maureen Keyes
University of Wisconsin—Madison
Madison, WI

James McLeskey
University of Florida
Gainesville, FL

Shirley Ritter
Furman University
Greenville, SC

Gina Scala
East Stroudsburg University
East Stroudsburg, PA

Tom Skrtic
University of Kansas
Lawrence, KS

About the Authors

Leonard C. Burrello is Professor of Education in the Department of Educational Leadership and Policy Studies and Executive Director of the *Forum on Education* at Indiana University. His work along with his mentor and coauthor Dan Sage, formerly of Syracuse University, is the longest and most consistent application of research on leadership and management related to inclusive school practices. Their three books have been the standard reference work in preparation programs for administrators in special services and at the school site. Dr. Burrello and Edith Beatty, a coauthor here, have recently completed their eighth major program evaluation study of special services from the Eastern Seaboard to the Midwest and Southwest. In addition to fieldwork in over 40 states and 120 school districts, Dr. Burrello chaired the Department of Education Leadership for 6 years, transforming its curriculum with the faculty of the School of Education from a managerial-technical perspective to one of transformational leadership. Besides teaching courses in school-level leadership and organizational change, Dr. Burrello directs the state director preparation program for the state of Indiana. At the *Forum on Education*, he has produced 11 videotapes on inclusion, coteaching (with Marilyn Friend), and standard-based reform and learner-centered schools.

Carl Lashley is Assistant Professor in the Department of Educational Leadership and Cultural Foundations at the University of

North Carolina at Greensboro. Dr. Lashley received his BA in Political Science and MA in Special Education from West Virginia University and his EdD in Educational Leadership from Indiana University, where Dr. Burrello served as his dissertation chair and mentor. Dr. Lashley has served as a general and special education teacher, elementary school principal, and general and special education administrator at the district level, all in rural central West Virginia. He directed the West Virginia Special Education Leadership Academy and has worked with teachers, administrators, and parents to promote inclusive and learner-centered practices in schools in West Virginia, Indiana, New York, and North Carolina. Dr. Lashley currently teaches courses in Educational Law and Special Education Leadership at UNC Greensboro and manages NC*IDEA (http://www.uncg.edu/elc), a Web site and discussion list that serves special education administrators in North Carolina. His research and advocacy interests are in the areas of disabilities policy, poverty and education, rural schools, and innovative modes of professional development for teachers and administrators.

Edith E. Beatty is Director of Vermont's Statewide System of Educator Preparation and Professional Development. Dr. Beatty has served as a teacher, local director of special education, professional developer, technical assistance provider, and program evaluator for more than 25 years. She earned her doctorate in Educational Leadership and Policy Studies at Indiana University. Her dissertation, portraying an individual incentives exchange within the marketplace of staff development, was the beginning of many studies, program evaluations, and national fieldwork with her mentor and colleague, Leonard Burrello. Dr. Beatty directed the Northeast Regional Resource Center, part of a federally supported national network of centers providing technical assistance to state and local agencies in special education throughout New England, New York, and New Jersey, She also directed the Institute for Program Development at Trinity College of Vermont, supporting a number of grants and programs in education and human services, including special education, community mental health, inquiry-based science, transition services, professional development and program evaluation. Prior to beginning her new post in statewide professional development, she was Research Associate Professor in the College of Education and Social Services at the University of Vermont and directed the

Best Practices Exchange. Over the past 6 years she has served on the Joint Committee on Standards for Educational Evaluation, representing the Association for Supervision and Curriculum Development, International. She is passionate about the work of systems change through reflective practice, continuous learning, and the thoughtful use of "good enough" data.

1

Students at the Margins

A tragedy is playing out in American schools. The joy of learning has been replaced by the monotony of control and standardization. The public schools have become places where children are either weeded out if they do not fit the school's mold or made to conform to arbitrary, oppressive standards and structures. Some students are categorized and placed in special programs (special education, bilingual education, alternative schools, etc.), because their learning needs cannot be met in the regular classroom. However, there are also significant numbers of uncategorized, unlabeled students for whom school is not about success in learning. For these students, school is somewhere they go because they have to. School does not foster their learning, nor does it challenge them to become independent workers or active citizens. School is where they go until they can go somewhere else to do that which is important to them. This is a dual tragedy: (a) Students are discouraged about learning because school does not appeal to them, and (b) the school is not able to nurture and challenge them in socially desirable directions because they are there only physically or not at all.

Today's students have more options for learning at their disposal outside of school, and they must learn to respond to social, economic, and technological situations that are simultaneously new and rapidly changing. Schools are not providing students with what they need to know and do in ways that are motivating or inspiring to young minds grappling with dynamic social conditions. Schools designed for the past poorly serve students in the present and poorly prepare them for life in the future, circumstances that are detrimental to students personally and to society collectively.

Schools and their leadership focus too much on the center—the majority of students who achieve and who have the attention of vocal parents, community patrons, or business patrons. If schools are interested in educating all students well, we contend that they must attend to the margins—those vulnerable students who have little parental guidance and no voice in school affairs. These students may come from a lower social class; have racial, ethnic, or ability differences; come from families that speak other languages; or have different social and religious customs. High-performing students also need the opportunity to test the margins. They too require teachers and peers who challenge them to think more deeply. All of these students are complex human systems who test the response systems educators typically use to foster learning and compliance with the rules and routines of the school day. These students challenge the curriculum and its standards, the teacher's normal instruction routines, and the motivational strategies that stimulate learning and compliance in the classroom. They present educators with a grand opportunity to create new learning for themselves and examine their invitation to learning for all students. These students constantly challenge the equilibrium and boundaries of the classroom and their diversity calls out for the school to change. They are the engines of reform.

The Change Context

Disequilibrium is a constant in living systems. Without disequilibrium, change is unnecessary. Wheatley (1997) describes disequilibrium in organizations, when she argues that living human systems are involved in a continuous dialectic in which they redefine themselves in relation to other living systems. She calls this phenomenon *complex adaptive systems*. We will contend here that schools are complex adaptive systems in which each student, each teacher, and each classroom interact with one another to redefine the future.

Looking at schools as complex adaptive systems reveals the need for school leaders and their constituents to engage everyone in learning, if the school is to redefine itself for a more effective future. Becoming responsible for their own learning while contributing to the learning needs of others means respecting and cooperating with all the diverse members of the school-community. Succeeding depends on one's capacity to adapt to the community and its contexts. Learning to manage the paradox of attending to individual needs while maintaining the community's viability is everyone's responsibility.

In the 20th century, American schools have been conceptualized as simple, stable, mechanical systems. The traditional response to student failure has been to create a separate subsystem of services for those students who do not fit into the dominant, "regular" system. These parallel systems have developed in response to federal legislation that was intended to remedy problems of inequity in public education by providing, remedial, compensatory, or special educational services for failing students. The Elementary and Secondary Education Act (ESEA, 1965) and Public Law 94-142 (1975), the Individuals with Disabilities Education Act (IDEA, 1997), and the Bi-Lingual Education Act are examples of such legislation. Because our area of greatest concern is students with disabilities, we are most familiar with the development of the parallel system of special education, which has been referred to as the "two box system" by Reynolds and Birch (1982).

Parallel systems shunt students who do not conform to the regular educational system into separate educational environments. The decision to change the placement of the student is made within what many educators believe are the best interests of the student. However, research about the effectiveness of separate systems and critical reflection about the assumptions that support this decision making (Skrtic, 1991) reveal that parallel systems are not an appropriate response to the problem of student failure. Perhaps the most disastrous consequence of placement in parallel systems is that it compartmentalizes responsibility for the education of these students. The school as an organization is relieved of responsibility for these students and as a result is not required to adapt itself to respond to their diversity.

Understanding schools as complex adaptive systems begins with valuing and taking responsibility for all students. School leaders must facilitate a school-community conversation that articulates that all students are valuable and can learn and that all students benefit when they are educated together. School leaders need to stand in the middle of the diversity in their school-communities and scan the environment to identify and advocate for the vulnerable children at the margins. Their task is to facilitate the development of the school-community's capacity to respond to diversity as it presents itself in the dynamic social environment. Their response is simultaneously moral and practical: Looking to the margins brings people into society who have been excluded, and working at the margins requires the organization to do things differently to be successful. Working at the margins fosters fairness and innovation.

The test for capacity building occurs at the margins. The next source of disequilibrium is just around the corner, and it rarely occurs in the center of the school organization. The school leader must engage the school-community in discourse about the moral, social, economic, and personal purposes of schooling to ensure that school decisions and programs are driven by a quest for both equity and excellence. Although many argue that equity and excellence are incompatible, a democratic society and the schools necessary for the fulfillment of its goals require that all children be provided with an education that prepares them to thrive in adulthood. Schools have historically excluded those students at the margins. To respond to the demands of the information age, free market, democratic society of the 21st century, schools must attend to students at the margins. Our moral commitment to educating all children demands this response, and our need to understand diversity to foster innovation requires it.

Complex Adaptive Systems

Complex Adaptive Systems (CAS) can be used as a set of perspectives, principles, and frameworks to guide district and school initiatives, replacing the more formal processes of strategic planning or *total quality management*, which have enjoyed widespread adoption but fleeting and questionable results in schools. CAS brings new insights to understanding organizational relationships in practice. We have used CAS perspectives to reflect on six specific program evaluation studies to help us understand the differences in educational contexts that require different decision-making options.

CAS and the learner-centered perspectives complement one another. Since both begin with the individual agent as a complex adaptive system, they accept the sociocultural history of the individual as unique and simultaneously expect and value the diversity that stems from the individual's unique experience. Both expect individuals to use their personal, learned experiences to find the means to solve problems collectively through work groups. CAS suggests that, when leadership outlines what a "good-enough vision" looks like without the details, work groups can interpret their meaning quite well and proceed to secure the technology and processes necessary to achieve the vision. CAS also suggests that the leaders need to outline standards of performance. Work groups will not only rise to the occasion and meet minimal expectations but will often exceed them.

The Policy/Politics Tension

Darling-Hammond (1993) offers two conflicting policy views that demand responses from educators and their critical publics. In the dominant view, policymakers believe that

> students are raw material to be "processed" by schools according to specifications dictated by schedules, programs, courses, and exit tests. Teachers administer the procedures to the students assigned to them, using the tools they are given: textbooks, curriculum guidelines, lists of objectives, course syllabi. Correctly defining the procedures is key to educational improvement. If the outcomes are not satisfactory, the solution is to provide more detailed prescriptions for practice and to monitor implementation more carefully. (p. 754)

Darling-Hammond (1993) argues for a position in which

> the assumptions that students are not standardized and that teaching is not routine. Consonant with recent research on teaching and learning, this view acknowledges that effective teaching techniques will vary for students with different learning styles, with differently developed intelligence, or at different stages of cognitive and psychological development; for different subject areas; and for different instructional goals. Far

from following standardized instructional packages, teachers must base their judgments on knowledge of learning theory and pedagogy, of child development and cognition, and of curriculum and assessment. They must then connect this knowledge to the understandings, dispositions, and conceptions that individual students bring with them to the classroom. (pp. 754-755)

The educational policy context is fraught with tension because it brings together aspirations for higher achievement for all students and limited capacities and resources. School boards feel these tensions when they deliberate about schools' efforts to achieve and maintain higher standards, and often the loudest voices they hear are those of parents who are demanding more sophisticated curriculum, advanced placement courses, or gifted pullout programs, all of which consume a disproportionate amount of resources while sustaining social class distinctions. Advocates for students who are unsuccessful in school are less often heard because they do not have the political and economic clout that accrues to middle- and upper-class families.

How schools come to the decisions they make is indicative of the power relations that exist in a community. As a result, national advocacy groups and the federal government have moved to improve educational equity and opportunity for historically underrepresented groups by passing legislation requiring that local school districts pay attention to the needs of unsuccessful students, regardless of how much power other voices have when they are mobilized around an educational issue. For many communities, Darling-Hammond's (1993) dominant perspective has served the needs of some students well, and that has been sufficient for that community. However, the alternative view, inspired by the aspiration for social equity and the need for universal high-quality education in a democracy, has been brought to the attention of schools by federal and state policy and the educational policy establishment.

An important aspect of this policy debate has been the role of the state in determining what students learn and how that learning is manifested. We recognize the attention that standards-based reform has brought to public education and appreciate its contributions. However, state- (or district-) level standards-based reform is not enough to ensure that schools educate all students equitably and excellently. State-driven, standards-based reform can result in reducing teacher discretion to individualize curriculum, instruction, and assessment to meet diverse learner needs. We suggest that schools adopt a learner-centered perspective in which students, their parents, and their teachers design annual personal educational plans that include appropriate standards to challenge the student. Standards-based reform has the advantage of getting all of the significant educational stakeholders to agree to valued outcomes. The contribution of learner-centered schools is that instruction and assessment are designed and implemented individually as means for the individual student to achieve those outcomes. Failure to meet standards is viewed as a design, implementation, or timing flaw to be corrected, rather than as a judgment about the student's ability to learn or his/her worth as a person to be used to determine the student's station in life.

A learner-centered schools approach requires that each student have a plan for learning and that she produce results that are evident to his/herself, to peers, and to teachers and parents. Managing one's time is part of the student planning and execution process, and these management skills have as much to do with future success as the content to be mastered. We have learned through our studies that inviting all students to assume more responsibility for their own learning changes the nature of student work in schools. The student becomes an inquirer who focuses on the appropriate selection of standards and rubrics for assessment and demonstrates her performance. Providing personalized education for all students renders moot the issue of including students who have been excluded. All students have diverse learning needs, and the core technologies of the school assume that diversity is valuable and integral to social life.

Managing Paradox

Managing paradox is fast becoming a most desirable leadership skill. In a society that celebrates the ascendancy of the individual, relegating students who learn differently to separate programs, classrooms, and schools is paradoxical. Shouldn't our valuing of individual perspectives, preferences, and differences extend to the classroom?

Besides presenting us with this moral and educational paradox, our thinking about diversity and education engenders many practical problems. Defining who fits and who doesn't uses valuable resources and alienates those who are singled out. For those who leave the mainstream, reentry is almost never satisfactory for the individual, his family, or peer group. Being relegated to a subsystem often means that expectations are lowered and that growth is stifled. The very subsystems that have been developed to help unsuccessful students have been shown to exacerbate their lack of success. Finally, subsystems are expensive. Because they engender bureaucratic duplication, they consume resources and lead to the conclusion that scarce resources are being used to provide programs that do not result in improved outcomes. As a result, the consumers of those programs—students—are blamed for both their lack of success in school and for consuming more resources than the blamecasters think they deserve. The contradiction in this argument is painfully obvious and is detrimental to students and to society: Unsuccessful students are blamed for the inability of the school to respond to their needs.

The successful leader is best advised to manage both dimensions of a paradox rather than to compromise either dimension for the sake of the other. Table 1.1 lists sets of paradoxes that school leaders face in their daily practice. These paradoxes are at the heart of stakeholder claims on the public schools and serve to keep schools from creating equity and opportunity for all students.

Leadership is a messy human drama with a diverse and complex plot. Paradoxes sow the seeds of discontent for school leaders. The work starts in the district office where policies and programs are chosen. District leaders cannot require that special education and regular education work together; they must develop a consensus that collaborative work makes sense for all concerned. An important centerpiece in that consensus is revisiting the purpose of schooling and identifying transcending purpose that gives meaning to education for all. Leaders must invite the public to revisit the purpose to examine whose interests are served by the way education is structured and delivered. Leaders must listen to the community and challenge it when what is being represented does not match either reality or the schools' aspirations for excellence and equity. School leaders must engage the public in a conversation about the future that

TABLE 1.1
Paradoxes in School Leadership

Think long-term	Deliver results now
Maintaining community	Meeting individual needs
Individual liberty	Collective security
Competition for top honors	Desire to see every student achieve
High test scores	Authentic learning
Homogeneous grouping	Heterogeneous grouping
Teacher as teaching and learning generalist	Teacher as teaching and learning specialist
Collaboration	Individual autonomy
Team responsibility and accountability	Individual responsibility and accountability
Meeting the individual needs of students	Teaching to a class norm
Functional leadership	Open and supportive leadership
Centralized decision making	Decentralized decision making
Expecting high levels of performance	Deferring to mediocrity
Responding to powerful constituents	Advocating for powerless constituents
Innovation	Stability
Embracing failure as an avenue to learning	Avoiding mistakes at all costs

includes an examination of traditional values, respect for the individual and his/her diversity, and the norms of belonging in the community.

Connecting Essential Concepts

This book connects three sets of concepts and perspectives about how school organizations actually work. The three concepts and their corresponding perspectives are drawn from the literature on complex adaptive systems (CAS), learner-centered schools (LCS), and unified systems of service delivery (US). We illustrate their relationship by using the following graphic:

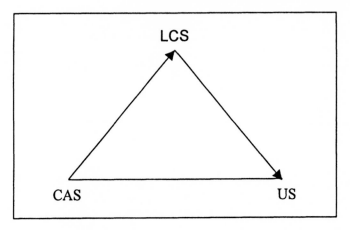

Complex adaptive systems (CAS) thinking helps explain how leaders actually lead and encourages followers to take ownership of their work in knowledge-based organizations. We believe schools as social learning organizations require that leaders act as framers of purpose and direction through "a good enough vision" and "minimum specifications." This is the same relationship that teachers should extend to their students' work.

Another concept from CAS, co-evolution, also impacts the teacher-student relationship. Teacher work and student work are inextricably bound together in a dynamic tension, stretching and contracting one another's viewpoints and contributions to their mutual learning. CAS and Unified Systems are the means to creating learner-centered schools, whose foundations in individual, developmental, and social learning theory require that the student as worker constructs his/her own learning in a co-evolutionary relationship with his/her teachers. Self-referencing assessment is the primary means to judge individual performance.

Unified systems complement the principles of CAS in that each concept requires both leadership and the faculty in a school to support student ownership of learning and teacher ownership of the responsibility to teach all children regardless of social class, race, gender, ethnicity, and disability or special need. All students are unique; some are more challenging than others. The public school system is purposeful in creating what Postman (1995) calls a "public" by including all of the public inside the schoolhouse door. In short, it takes all three sets of concepts to think about how learning occurs, how learners relate to one another, and how leaders, faculty, and students connect to create learning settings and opportunities that are unpredictable, limitless, and enriching for all.

Essential Questions Guiding a
Unified System of Leadership

As some of our students were studying a draft of this book with us, they asked: (a) How are the concepts are connected? and (b) What is the leadership challenge for any school administrator who is arguing for a change in the delivery of services to vulnerable students in a school or school district? In proper professorial fashion, we responded by providing a set of operationalizing questions. Our questions are:

1. What is the purpose of education? What are we trying to achieve for all students? This question is the most fundamental and yet the one most of us take for granted. We provide some insight about our perspectives on the answer in the next chapter.

2. What is school success, and how it is measured for all students? How do we demonstrate success for students with special needs? What standards are we being held accountable for that measure achievement, personal/social growth, and post-school success? How are students with special needs performing compared to their typical peers? This set of questions immediately suggests two things: (a) Who wants to know if students with special needs are succeeding? and (b) Do special educators have a set of learning standards that guides their practice?

3. What do we envision students with special needs doing in school to prepare for post-school life? How is their education more the same than different from their typical peers? This perspective argues for similarity of outcomes and treatment, rather than difference, and an outcome orientation first and foremost.

4. In what ways are general education staff responsible to educate all students including those with special needs? How are special educators held accountable for assisting general educators in meeting their responsibility to educate all students? How can special education personnel ever be perceived as equal by their peers, if they are not being held accountable for student performance as their peers

are? We have come to believe, through our extensive program evaluation efforts in six states, that unless teachers and school site leaders assume responsibility for all students, students with special needs will always be marginalized.

5. How do we as educators justify our practice? How do special services personnel impact the capacity of staff and schools to educate students with diverse needs? Are their practices meritorious? Do the practices demonstrate worth in the minds of others? Special services can no longer survive under the guise of mandatory legislation. The test in education now is to demonstrate how to differentiate instruction and illustrate its impact on student growth.

6. What framing policies and practices need to be in place to support the concept of a unified system that includes all students including those with special needs? How are they aligned with other district and state policies? Can the protection and due process procedures needed to ensure parental and student rights be understood and used successfully by school level leadership without the direct intervention of district personnel? Few school systems we have worked with have explicit policies that speak to these issues. We have the data on student achievement and corresponding exemplary practices that support a unified system framework. Generating the will to make them explicit and demonstrating to staff the need for change are the essential leadership tasks.

7. Does the leadership in the district support school-level planning and problem-solving that lead to generative learning? Are the minimum specifications clear so that the school site teams can plan, design, and implement appropriate programs of study for all students with special needs? The orientation of district leadership from the Board and superintendent of schools requires a vision of services that are more the same for all than different. The role of top leadership is to paint the vision and provide the parameters that support the work of teaching and learning envisioned for all students.

8. What are we learning as educators, and how are we sharing that learning with all staff the community at large? Education has been largely a private practice. Special service personnel are making it a public practice by entering those classrooms and demonstrating how to differentiate instruction and how to use learners as the best role models for their peers. Unless we learn how to customize learn-

ing for each student, we can never achieve our goals of equity and excellence for all students.

We have been described as Pollyannas because we believe that equity and excellence can be achieved simultaneously. We have been to schools and worked with teachers and administrators who use the approaches we recommend with considerable success. Their stories are woven throughout this book. We are realists. We know that schools face difficult, complex challenges and that creating a good school is a tough task for those courageous souls who believe an excellent education for all students is worth the trouble.

2

Reconceiving the Purposes
of Schooling

Educating young people is an invitation to explore with them who they are and what they want to become. Adults have an interest in the educative process because they want children to have a good life. Children are naturally interested in the world around them and in their futures. Together, adults and children have a responsibility to make the most of an education, both as an act of self-interest and as an investment in their collective social futures.

Inasmuch as education is a social act, it requires that students come to understand one another, treat one another with civility and respect, and learn to manage their individual wants and desires. Coming together in schools and classrooms creates opportunities for students to engage in intellectual, social, and moral experiences from which they learn the lessons of life that will carry them into adulthood. Each student is a complex human system with his/her own sociocultural history that provides a built-in radar screen with which the student scans his environment to locate those things that are important to him/her. As s/he encounters new ideas, new tools, and other people, his learning task becomes one of identifying and negotiating common goals and shared norms that will enhance his/her participation in society.

Public schools offer many students their first opportunity for membership in a public enterprise (Postman, 1995). Following the rules is an obligation of membership, but learning how to respond to the collaborative responsibilities of membership is an important, ongoing lesson for students as they serve their apprenticeship as citizens and workers. Their success at learning the responsibilities of membership will affect their postschool adjustment in society and in the workplace. In short, the purpose of public schools is to create a public (Postman, 1995). School is about preparing children to participate and contribute to that public as citizens in a democracy.

Teachers and principals, superintendents and board members, community members and business people must recognize that innovations such as changing structures to increase time on tasks (e.g., block scheduling, after-school tutoring, summer school), teaming (multidisciplinary teams, team teaching), and teacher empowerment (collaboration, site-based management) are important but not sufficient to change practice in the significant ways that are necessary to transform schooling so that all children are educated for full participation in society. Students are incredibly diverse and are becoming more so. A differentiated approach is necessary to do what our democratic, moral purposes and our practical, social and economic goals require—that we educate all students to levels of excellence that sustain both their personal growth and our social fabric.

School communities are hampered in their efforts to provide a differentiated education for all students. They do not have examples, symbols, or representations available to help them reimagine their schools. Postman (1995) has used narratives and metaphors to stimulate new thinking about schools, and we have used his approaches to engage school-communities in discussions about their futures. After a discussion of Postman's approaches, we will turn to some discursive materials we have used to engage schools in efforts to reimagine themselves as unified systems that respond to the needs of all students.

Postman's Narratives to Guide Education
and to Create Community Life

Narratives are vehicles for translating the purposes of social enterprises. Narratives pervade cultures; they provide the great ideas toward which people aspire and the guidance necessary to reach those aspirations. In a world that seeks objective solutions and recipes for quality, narratives can provide an ennobling vision that synthesizes the real and the ideal into credible and complex understanding (Postman, 1995). In his book, *The End of Education* (1995), Postman asks who creates the narratives that bind a nation and give purpose and meaning to the idea of a public education. Sometimes, educators are captivated by one narrative or another; at other times, they do not have any narrative at all to bind them to American society. Postman argues that the purpose of narrative is to give meaning to the world, not to describe it scientifically. "The measure of a narrative's 'truth' or 'falsity' is in its consequences: Does it provide people with a sense of personal identity, a sense of community life, a basis for moral conduct, explanations of that which cannot be known?" (p. 7).

American educators have attached themselves to the social and economic narratives that dominate the American landscape. According to Postman (1995), the major narratives—"some gods that fail"—that currently guide American society are these:

- Efficiency, which leads many local business interests and free market and school voucher advocates to believe that market competition enhances the productivity and performance of schools
- Technology, which drives the international computer and telecommunication industry and many Wall Street market makers and which would replace the existing human system of education with the latest in teaching technologies
- Economic utility, which leads many parents and students to believe that schools are primarily about economic survival and vocational aspirations significant to industrialists in manufacturing, technology, banking, sales, marketing, and many boards of education

- Consumerism, which argues that "whoever dies with the most toys wins" (p. 33)
- Separatism or tribalism, which leads racial and ethnic factions to promote their own cultural and linguistic heritage

These "gods that fail" share the assumption that society is served by an educational and social system that sorts its citizens. For those who tell these stories, there will always be "haves and have-nots" and a system for determining into which group children will fit. Separating students by ability, however it may be defined, is an appropriate social function because it is in both the student's and society's best interest. Education is the vehicle in which this sorting begins (Spring, 1989). Those who articulate these narratives support sorting students by ability to provide a variety of opportunities for them. Examples include homogeneous grouping and tracking, vocational education, and single-race or -gender schools. These narratives fail because they compartmentalize difference and thereby fragment society.

Postman (1995) offers five narratives—"gods that may serve"—to extend our view of ourselves in the world. These narratives can provide us with a symbolic landscape from which schools can exercise their dual purposes—to teach children to accept and simultaneously to question the culture as it is and as it should be:

The Spaceship Earth. The people of earth must join together in interdependence and global cooperation. All inhabitants suffer when the resources of the Spaceship Earth are squandered. A shared vision of the future and a global commitment to the present must develop for the planet to survive. The purpose of schooling, then, is to provide children with an understanding of their connections to others.

The Fallen Angel. All human beings make mistakes all the time, and it is natural that we do. However, we are capable of redemption; that is, we can all improve and fix our mistakes. Postman (1995) adds, "Knowing that we do not know and cannot know the whole truth, we may move toward it inch by inch by discarding what we know to be false. And then watch the truth move farther and farther away" (p. 66). The purpose of schooling is to "cure the itch for absolute knowledge" (p. 70) so that children understand the implications of their inherent imperfectability.

The American Experiment. This narrative began with Lincoln's challenge to American society to deal with the ideal in the "American Creed"—a government of the people, by the people, and for the people. According to Postman (1995), the most fundamental question posed by this narrative is, "Can a nation be formed, maintained, and preserved on the principle of continuous argumentation?" (p. 73). The purpose of schooling is "to provide our youth with the knowledge and will to participate in the great experiment; to teach them how to argue, and to help them discover what questions are worth arguing about; and of course, to make sure they know what happens when arguments cease" (pp. 73-74).

The Law of Diversity. The American narrative is a story in which people from many cultures come together to form a common culture. This narrative has been used both productively—to build common bonds between individuals and groups—and negatively—to fragment and separate Americans and to seek revenge for past discrimination. Postman (1995) goes on to say that we must learn from the significant contributions of people from all cultural groups to see "how the vitality of humanity and creativity depend upon diversity and because they have set the standards to which civilized adhere. The law of diversity thus makes intelligent humans of us all" (p. 81).

The Word Weavers/The World Makers. Language and the way it creates the world we come to know is the driving force behind what makes us human. As Postman (1995) describes it, "When we form a sentence, we are creating a world. We are organizing it, making it pliable, understandable, useful. In the beginning, there was the word, and in the end as well" (p. 84). The purpose of schooling, then, is to provide children with the mastery of language as the currency for the moral and social dimensions of the culture.

These narratives provide us with a base from which we can develop theories and practices of schooling. Although some doubt whether the public school can survive, Postman (1995) makes a strong case that "no one has made a better way to create a public" (p. 197). Schools, and the constituencies they serve and support, must begin to understand these and other narratives about the society in which we live, and they must develop their own subnarratives that explore the purposes of schools and initiatives to change them.

Educational leaders, like their counterparts in other public spheres, have failed to address the most fundamental issue—defining the purpose of the public school (Postman, 1995). Educators are responsible for developing an informed and responsible public. All students are learners and citizens who live in our communities. They are and will be the public our society inherits. They will not go away even if we try to send them. Public school ought to be a place where students learn to live in a democracy where all voices are heard. Postman calls this the *American experiment*, and our contribution to the debate about the purposes of schooling is the development of three discourses about the education of students with disabilities that provide historical, contemporary, and emergent ways of thinking about school organizational designs that support the American experiment.

Three Discourses About Educating Students With Disabilities

The history of the education of students with disabilities is a story about efforts to move them from the margins of education to sharing the center. We have organized this story into three discourses to indicate that creating progressively more inclusive educational programs for students with disabilities has been the hallmark of the history of special education (Reynolds & Birch, 1982; Skrtic, 1991). Figure 2.1 represents the discourses graphically. We believe that the history and practices of special education provide an interesting and useful vantage point from which to criticize efforts to improve education for all students and to achieve important social ends.

The Continuum of Services

The context of special education prior to the passage of EHA/ IDEA[1] was one of separation for those students who received special

Figure 2.1. Discourses in Special Education

Dominant	Transitional	Emergent
EHA/Mainstreaming The Continuum of Services embodied in EHA/IDEA	REI/Inclusion Inclusive Schools Effective schools research, critique of EHA/mainstreaming models	Unified Schools Learner-Centered Schools Complex adaptive systems
Grounding Assumptions: • Disabilities are inherent in children • Differential diagnosis is useful • Special education is a rational and coordinated system • Diagnosis and identification are necessary to secure resources and services	**Grounding Assumptions:** • All children can learn • All children should be educated in their neighborhood schools and communities • Schools must accommodate to meet the needs of students with disabilities • School personnel require ongoing professional renewal	**Grounding Assumptions:** • All children have a natural capacity for learning • All children construct their own knowledge • Schools must become learning centers for all members of the community • Increasingly diverse learners require differentiated instructional approaches • All students have personal learning plans • All student performance is authentic and demonstrable
Authority: functionalism, bureaucratic professionalism	Authority: critical theory, cultural studies	Authority: pragmatism, new science, adhocratic collaboration

SOURCE: (Adapted from Skrtic, 1991)

Passage of EHA	Will's REI proposals	APA Learner-Centered Principles
1975	1984	1995

BOX 2.1
Discourse One:
The Continuum of Services

Children come to school with varying abilities, motivation,
and life experiences. When these internal factors cause them
to fail in school, it is the school district's responsibility to
provide a continuum of remedial, compensatory, and special
services to meet their needs. Some students (those with
disabilities) have such extraordinary needs that it is
sometimes necessary to separate them from their peers to
meet those needs. Generating resources necessary to support
these services requires identifying students with labels such
as at-risk, remedial, disabled, or bilingual. Specialists have
developed tools and strategies to assess and plan for these
students, and separate settings have been established in
which their extraordinary needs can be met. Specially
trained personnel, working in specially designed and
delivered programs, are available to provide the remediation
and compensatory instruction that afford these students
equitable educational opportunities.

---

education. A disorganized system of disjointed services was supported by various public and private social institutions. The knowledge tradition in special education, which supported the services,
was an amalgam of knowledge from the practices of medicine, psy-
chiatry, and behavioral psychology. This knowledge tradition
treated disabilities as conditions that individuals have that distinguish them from their normal peers.

With the passage of EHA in 1975, the continuum of services
became the accepted model for providing special education services. The text in Box 2.1 summarizes the principles of the continuum of services.

As a result of the assumptions that support the continuum of services discourse, students with disabilities were separated from their
peers through the development of a parallel system of special education services. EHA/IDEA does not require the development of a parallel system of education, but certain assumptions about persons

with disabilities in concert with legal provisions have encouraged school districts and states to develop parallel systems for delivering required services to students with disabilities. Skrtic (1991) describes the grounding assumptions from the knowledge tradition of special education, which undergirds the continuum of services, as follows:

1. Disabilities are pathological conditions that students have.
2. Differential diagnosis is objective and useful.
3. Special education is a rationally conceived and coordinated system of services that benefits diagnosed students.
4. Progress results from incremental technological improvements in diagnosis and instructional interventions. (p. 54)

Proponents of the continuum of services also argue that a fifth principle is necessary for programs to secure the resources necessary to operate them: Differential diagnosis and labeling of students are necessary to prove to policymakers that there are students who need special attention and that funds will be used to address their specific needs.

Schools have been very successful in identifying a large number of students who have not learned the prescribed curriculum or prospered socially with their peers. Their solution to these dysfunctional students has been to separate them into special classes and service configurations staffed by specialists with training that is derived from clinical psychology and a medical model that prescribes student pathology. The parallel system is the "two box approach" (Reynolds & Birch, 1982) come home to roost in American public schools, and its cost and effectiveness have been called into question by policymakers, administrators, researchers, and educators from the general and special education disciplines.

Inclusive Schools

During the 1980s, researchers and government officials wrote extensively about the need to abolish the parallel delivery system for special education services to meet the educational needs of all students. These responses, variously named the Regular Education Initiative (REI), the Shared Responsibility Initiative, and the Inclusive

BOX 2.2
Discourse Two:
Inclusive Schools

All students should be educated in the regular classroom, unless specific circumstances cause educators to place them in other educational environments. All students should attend the school to which they would normally go if they had no disability. Students with disabilities are distributed in their natural proportion at the school site in regular education programs that are age and grade appropriate. No students are denied placement at the school site on the basis of the severity of disability unless they are a danger to themselves or others. Special education support services are primarily provided within the context of the regular education program in addition to other cooperative learning and peer support practices. Students are assured of an equitable and appropriate education when they are educated together.

Schools Movement, have been offered as alternatives to the parallel system and the continuum of services model.

According to Skrtic (1991), those who participated in the debate over mainstreaming "argued for greater access to the general education program within the traditional organizational configuration of schools" (p. 56). The circumstances of the times supported the mainstreaming/EHA model, because implementation of the model allocated the resources necessary to support the practice of special education. "In the end, the mainstreaming/EHA model (and its associated practices and tools) emerged as the solution . . . not because it was conceptually sound, but because, morally and politically, it was the right thing to do" (p. 57).

Rhetoric has shifted to the use of the term *inclusion* to describe those efforts to overcome the inadequacies of the continuum of services by educating more students with disabilities in the regular classroom. Proponents of inclusion have called for a merged system of services that will bring regular and special education together to meet the needs of students who have a history of school failure. The

the inclusive schools discourse (Gartner & Lipsky, 1989; Sailor, 1991). The inclusive schools movement has been particularly criticized, because it has not aligned with other initiatives in changing schools to improve their responsiveness to the needs of all students. The learning-centered schools discourse represents an attempt to merge the technologies, outcomes, and work relationships associated with inclusive schools with efforts to provide equity and excellence in educational opportunities for all students.

In 1992, the Center for Policy Options in Special Education published a monograph titled *Issues and Options in Special Education* (McLaughlin & Warren, 1992), which served as the basis for the development of the CASE Future Agenda (1992). These approaches recommend the creation of a unified system that serves the needs of all students equitably and excellently. As we have worked with these approaches, it has become apparent that the continuum of services and the inclusive schools discourses are insufficient to depict the emerging leadership challenge for school site and district leaders. A third discourse has arisen as a result of our consideration of a unified systems approach, and it is summarized in Box 2.3.

The assumptions that ground this discourse are these:

All Children Have a Natural Capacity for Learning. Proponents of learner-centered schools argue that not only can all students learn but that all children do learn because learning is natural to them. Given this assumption, schools must provide multiple environments that stimulate and motivate all students regardless of their capacity for or style of learning.

All Children Construct Their Own Knowledge. Learning occurs naturally when students are encouraged to create responses that solve problems and reveal knowledge that is important to them. Students learn when they are able to use the knowledge they have to acquire and understand new information. Students must be encouraged to make connections in their learning and to build conceptual networks that allow them to relate ideas and to think critically.

Schools Must Become Learning Centers for All Members of the Community. Students need to see models of learning exhibited by adults. Adults need to learn constantly in order to respond cre-

---

BOX 2.3
Discourse Three:
Learning-Centered Schools

All students have special needs, although some are more unusual than others. It is not necessary to label or separate students in order to provide them with an appropriate education, and excellence in education is accomplished when all children are educated together. The primary needs for all students are to learn to live, work, and participate in the community, since the community is where life occurs. Education for life after school should begin in the neighborhood school and successively expand to the community at large. When teachers with varying expertise work collaboratively and use a variety of strategies and technologies, they can address the needs of all students. Students and other members of the school community benefit when they work together daily to meet those individual and diverse needs. Achieving educational equity and excellence requires unifying all members of the school community around a vision and set of outcomes for all students. Placing students at the center of the enterprise becomes the common focus and common task of all members of the school community.

---

atively to the demands of students. Providing an environment that nurtures learning for all its constituencies requires that schools reach out into communities to build learning networks and bridges to understanding.

Increasingly Diverse Learners Require Increasingly Diverse Educational Strategies. Because children come to school with increasingly diverse backgrounds and experiences, their previously acquired knowledge is highly differentiated. Providing an environment in which students can construct learning requires that the school provide a broad array of curriculum, instructional, and assessment strategies to ensure that all students have the fullest opportunity to reach their maximum potential.

All Students Have Personal Learning Plans. A school program that capitalizes on all children's natural capacity for learning and celebrates their diversity must by its very nature be individualized. This individualization must be purposefully and collaboratively designed and implemented to ensure that all perspectives about the student are honored and nurtured. Getting students to assume increasing responsibility for planning and implementing their personal plans with their parents, peers, and teachers is the hallmark of this discourse. A system of personal learning plans also changes educators' perspectives of the child and focuses the school on the individual student rather than groups.

All Student Performance Is Authentic and Demonstrable. Assessment results are shared with all appropriate stakeholder groups to influence individual teacher and student planning, within-group planning within the classroom, and between teams of teachers within a grade level and between grade levels.

These assumptions come from philosophical pragmatism and constructivism. They assume that learning is an interactive, social phenomenon that has democratic dialogue at its roots. This discourse builds on the inclusive schools discourse because it also assumes that all students should be educated together and that learning is the core service the school provides. However, it departs from the inclusive schools discourse when it argues for individualization for each learner, including those adults who are part of the school community—teachers, administrators, parents, and community patrons. It recognizes that each child's interest in learning creates a diverse system of learners to which the school has an obligation to respond.

The learner-centered schools concept suggests that the teacher seek to personalize education for each student, that students thrive on group study and reflection, cooperative work groups, and project learning. Since all students learn differently, they should be educated in classrooms that respect diversity and build on the qualities that all students bring with them to school. Students with disabilities in this discourse are individuals with complex adaptive capacities, just like every other complex person in the classroom. They can all benefit from direct access to the general education curriculum, their natural peer group, and teachers who know that curriculum best.

Some students might need some accommodations and modifications in instruction to be successful, but they will perform to higher standards when they are educated in high-expectation environments.

Tinkering at the Margins

American schooling has been about moving groups of students from one classroom to the next, sorting and selecting them on the basis of merit. The teacher has been entrusted to do the right thing with his/her time in the classroom and then to hand off the group to another teacher. Today's movement toward the standardization of outcomes is an effort to enforce some form of quality control on what happens in the classroom. Standardization, external motivation, and high-stakes assessment are the hallmarks of current efforts to improve education's capacity to perform the sorting and selecting function that was its province in 20th-century America (Spring, 1989). Howe (1995) argues that state intervention to ensure student learning represents a shift from states' specifying the structures and inputs of schooling to their mandating the strategic processes that schools use to teach students. Although it has often been couched in decentralizing terms, state intervention in the 1990s securely fortified the state's authority over what occurs in the classroom.

The passage of EHA introduced alternative approaches for sorting and selecting to American schools, while requiring that educators attend to procedural fairness and the individual needs of students. Special education has been about assessing student learning potential and achievement to determine how individual students learn and adapt to their school, their peers, and the larger community's social and work expectations. These practices assume that learning is not routine and that it occurs in a social context, thus encouraging schools to look at each student as an individual. Although this focus could have reoriented schools to focus curriculum and instruction on the needs of students as individuals, its result has been the proliferation of disability labels, separation of students into special education service configurations, and fragmentation of the educational process for all students.

Note

1. We use the term EHA to represent the Education for All Handicapped Children Act of 1975. IDEA is used to represent EHA's successor, which was passed in 1990. We use the designation IDEA 97 to represent the reauthorization of IDEA that occurred in 1997. IDEA 97 deserves special designation because it includes several revisions that are significant for the development of unified systems of general and special education.

3

A Transformational Leadership Strategy

Complex Adaptive Systems

Traditional management theory has focused on rational and linear thinking about how organizations work, emphasizing predictability and control of people and processes. The metaphor for organizations in traditional theory is mechanical, a smooth-running machine like a clock. In this mechanical model, the emphasis is on efficiency, precision, regularity, order, and reliability. Management achieves these outcomes through the division of labor and the hierarchical supervision of production. Organizations become efficient and effective in achieving their goals by dividing labor into discrete tasks and delegating the work to highly specialized workers who perform the same tasks over and over again. The coordination of work is the task of management, not the workers. An organizational form that is patterned after the mechanical model is the bureaucracy.

Many researchers have applied the mechanical model to schools. Skrtic (1991) uses an analysis of schools as professional bureaucracies to contrast general and special education. In his view, general education is a professional bureaucracy that uses division of labor (e.g., organization into grades, subject specializations) and standardization of programs and skills (e.g., aligned curriculum, standardized tests) within a hierarchical structure to achieve organizational goals. As a result of its organization, the professional bureaucracy produces exceptions and failures—students who cannot succeed in a program of standardization and uniform performance. To circumscribe student failure, a professional bureaucracy creates special subsystems into which students who cannot succeed in the general system are placed. Special education is the subsystem that has been organized to contain the problem of student failure for those students who have disabilities.

Educational Organizations as Complex Adaptive Systems

Complexity science studies the patterns of relationships within organizations and how they function. Complex science invites us to examine the unpredictable, disorderly, and unstable aspects of organizational life. Metaphors like organisms or the brain more fittingly depict the complexities of organizations. Complex adaptive systems are everywhere—from the human body to the stock market, from forest ecosystems to the public schools (Wheatley, 1992).

Our understanding of complex science has led to our examination of educational organizations as complex adaptive systems. Systems are connected, interdependent, interacting agents—people and organizations with things to do. Schools are systems of people who are organized to create opportunities for learning. By complex, we mean that the organizations in our society charged with learning are diverse, complicated systems that connect with a large number of agents, both within and outside the system, all of which influence the purposes, goals, and success of the school. When we use the term *adaptive*, we mean that schools, and those agents touched by them, are systems that have the capacity to change, to learn from experience, and to alter their interactions with the agents that engage in exchanges with them.

Educational organization, as complex adaptive systems, are composed of interacting agents who follow rules, apply mental models, and exchange influence within their local communities and in response to the social environment, thereby altering the very environments they respond to simply by acting. Using complex adaptive systems as a lens for examining schools involves considering the exchanges that occur in the school and between the school and its community. Five linked attributes or properties characterize complex adaptive systems.

Interrelationships

Complex adaptive systems are embedded in other complex adaptive systems. Each individual agent in a system is a complex adaptive system in and of itself. Agents coevolve with systems. In schools, students coevolve with teachers and with each other; departments coevolve with teachers and with the school as a whole; the school coevolves with the departments and with the district. Agents independently evolve and simultaneously develop interdependence. The environment is synergistic—it is characterized by rigorous interchanges among people and, as a result, it fosters growth.

Diversity

Diversity is necessary to sustain a complex adaptive system. Information and innovation are essential for its long-term viability. Variation should be amplified rather than driven out of the system. In traditional schools, the emphasis is on control and uniformity, but learners have diverse interests, abilities, and needs. Educators continually struggle with this paradox. For example, the need to create safe schools requires order and control, but successful classrooms capitalize on the diversity of students and their coevolution with one another and their teachers. Another paradox is that a global, information-based society requires the critical thinking and problem-solving skills of its citizens, but current thinking in schools focuses on competition over test scores and international comparisons of student achievement. The drive for standardization suppresses the diversity that makes schools interesting and responsive learning environments for students, teachers, and communities.

Nonlinearity

Complex adaptive systems are nonlinear, and as such they hold within themselves a vast potential for transformation. Ettinger (1999) has outlined six factors that pinpoint the differences and contrast between nonlinearity and linear systems thinking:

1. Change in nonlinear thinking is precipitous and revolutionary, whereas change in linear systems is gradual and incremental. For example, strategic planning might create a plan for modifying instructional processes in a piecemeal fashion, whereas looking at the curriculum and its interrelationships might yield a new interdisciplinary approach.

2. Size of the effect is disproportionate to the cause in nonlinear system thinking although it is directly proportional in linear systems. For example, a strategic planning retreat might produce no change, whereas the whisper of gossip about inclusion causes a great backlash.

3. The whole is the sum of the parts in linear systems, but the whole is greater than sum of its parts in nonlinear systems because they are embedded and interactive. This gives the system potential beyond that of any one part. Outcomes are derived from the patterns of interrelationships more than the individual talents or capacities of any one agent. The system cannot be understood by reducing it to its parts. For example, schools cannot be reduced to the individual teachers and their classrooms. Student performance is an interdependent phenomenon that is a function of teacher, student, family, and community interactions (Leithwood & Aitken, 1995).

4. The elements in nonlinear systems interact multidirectionally and mutually, but interactions in linear systems are unidirectional. In complexity science, coevolution refers to the changing nature of relationships between agents and the growth that results. Our experience indicates that changing power relationships in classrooms, and thereby emphasizing mutual, multidirectional interactions, is the key catalyst for the transformation to a learner-centered school. Coevolution illustrates the tightly coupled relationship between the

teacher and student. Their mutual success depends how each interacts with the other.

5. Predictability of outcomes is uncertain in nonlinear systems, whereas linear systems strive for predictable outcomes and alignment of processes with resources and standard outcomes. Complex adaptive-systems thinking has taught us that the interactions among school agents that produce thought and discourse about standard outcomes create opportunities for growth among teachers and students. However, the standardization of outcomes does not produce higher achievement; rather, relationships and interactions create richer opportunities for learning and more responsiveness to classroom diversity, which in turn stimulate learning and achievement.

6. The potential for growth is considerable when conditions are unstable. In linear systems, change or growth is limited because the systems seek a return to stability and equilibrium, which results in replication of the status quo and drives out disturbance. Most organizations change at the margins, where problems, creativity, dissonance, and dissatisfaction percolate instability. Promising practices, such as cooperative learning, peer tutoring, personalization of education, and educational authenticity, have arisen when educators recognized that students at the margins were not being successfully educated.

Self-Organization

When complexity is allowed to emerge, self-organization takes place. In nonlinear systems, change is a self-generated and self-guided practice that is neither hierarchically controlled nor externally driven. Nonlinear thinking releases the system's participants' self-organizing potential to meet the challenge they face. Within and across schools, communities of people, who meet to inquire and discuss their concerns, will formulate change and learn to consider the context of the system. Skrtic (1991) calls this organizational mode *adhocracy* and suggests that schools should organize themselves as centers of inquiry in which learning to think, learn, and collaborate are the primary activities in which students engage. Linear thinking causes schools to suppress students' individual initiative and joy of learning because they are taught that they have no power over their education and that they will not learn what is important unless they are compelled by extrinsic motivation.

Attractors

Attractors are patterns or areas that draw system energy and define behaviors and their boundaries. Attractors create norms that direct the behavior of agents in the organization. In a learner-centered school, students and teachers are attracted by the pattern of behavior that follows when students assume responsibility for determining their own learning plans. For teachers, the attractor is more time spent facilitating learning and less time controlling off-task student behavior.

Complex adaptive systems are characterized by interrelationships, diversity, nonlinearity, self-organization, and attractors. To be successful at capitalizing on the elements and their understandings of complexity and adaptation, leaders have organized the resources at their disposal as learner-centered schools. Our work in schools using learner-centered principles has given us some insight into the leadership and organizational forms that are evident in these schools.

Leadership in Complex Adaptive Systems

The concept of complex adaptive systems is derived from the study of relationships between agents, their motivation, and their control of learning (Zimmerman, 1999). The leader who uses complex adaptive systems as a lens must consider context and relationships. At a time when relationship management is a key leadership skill, complex adaptive-systems thinking offers some new insights into how to transform education through a study of the context of learning and organizational theory. A radical leverage point and attractor for teachers is the role that students take in motivating themselves and being responsible for learning in the classroom. Leaders must consider five contextual issues as they work to transform their schools.

The Mental Model of Learning

The mental model of learning and the role of students take in learning changes in learner-centered schools. Power relationships become more democratic as students and teachers take control of their work in school. The more informed and independent the learner, the less direct instruction from the teacher is needed and the less control is required. Teachers help arrange the conditions for student learning to occur—like the farmer who doesn't make his crops grow but creates the conditions that help them grow. Redistributing who writes the constitution for the classroom from teacher alone to both teacher and students is the starting point.

State and Local Standards

The teacher's understanding of state and local standards and the assurance that student assessments are aligned with those standards influences the teaching and learning technologies the school uses to meet the needs of all students. Teachers, students, and parents must expect engagement in instruction that will lead to demonstrated competency. If students are expected to know and interpret those standards in light of both their meaning for themselves and how those standards will be assessed, they will develop an ownership for them from the beginning of their learning. If standards are to be effective tools in improving student learning, they must become widely understood by students, teachers, administrators, parents, and community members. Standards referred to as bars to hurdle have little meaning for anyone, whereas standards that describe learning and that are understood as applicable to a student's future can be used to motivate students and stimulate their interest in learning.

Supporting Teaching

Teachers must be supported as they learn and apply their learning in schools. To do their jobs successfully, teachers are expected to know everything about their students' sociocultural history, how they learn, and what support they will need to learn what is expected. Their students, the content, and social demands are increasingly more diverse. In the current work-alone, autonomous teaching model of schooling, these factors make the teacher's jobs overwhelming. Teachers can no longer be expected to work in private. They need time to collaborate and share their interpretations of what is expected of them and their students. This collaboration extends into their classrooms where teachers should expect in-class support from their colleagues and other specialized personnel. Teachers should be members of a variety of classroom, school, and district teams. As members of classroom teams, they share responsibility for meeting selected student outcomes with students and other teachers. As members of school teams, they build learning opportunities with their follow teachers. As members of their district team, they may be designing specifications for the district knowledge management system to ensure its meaningfulness and usefulness for them.

Teachers' Self-Organizing

Given an understanding of the purpose of schooling and the minimum specifications for which they are responsible, teachers will learn to manage themselves and the other resources they have at their disposal to support student learning. Teacher teams increase their use of resources and capacities to student learning in direct proportion to their capacity to demonstrate how they will continually improve their practice. The key relationship for district-level support staff and central office leadership to observe is how teacher teams are preparing themselves to get better. Personal, team, and school improvement plans must contain evidence of how students and adults will continue to learn. How they represent that learning and how it will be shared throughout the district are key assessment issues for district-level reform and transformation.

District Leadership and Support

District-level personnel and board members are responsible for designing and supporting continual improvement toward the district's benchmarks, its values, purposes, vision, and core technologies. This includes maintaining and sustaining the schools' relationships with important stakeholders and constituents and their claims on the district's vision and resources. District leaders must scout out the moral and social context of the school-communities, advocate for resources and support for schools, and hold schools accountable for their progress. Their jobs are both logistical and educative. They need to master the technical processes (accreditation, raising revenue, policy development, implementation, and accountability) necessary to make resources available, and they must teach the public about the purposes of schooling and its importance in a democratic society.

Leading in the Zone of Complexity

Stacey (1996) has argued that organizations range from mechanical to chaotic. Planning and control are appropriate for simple, mechanistic organizations; chaotic organizations should be avoided. In the range between the two resides an array of complex systems that requires new ways of thinking about organizing them for success. Zimmerman (1999) suggests that complexity science is useful for this thinking when issues are relatively complex. Simpler issues can be managed quite successfully through consensus, standardization, or delegation. The degree of certainty about the future and the level of agreement about action plans among stakeholders drive the use of complexity science. The "zone of complexity" provides the real opportunity for innovation to occur, since traditional responses and strategic planning methodologies are not perceived to be adequate for successful resolution of complex issues.

Complexity science principles have helped us understand how school leaders create self-organization and continuous adaptation to their environments—elements that are crucial to meeting the needs of all students in today's schools. We believe that understanding the culture of schools and the process of reculturing the public schools develop with the application of complex systems thinking and yield important guidance that can be used to transform bureaucratic schools into learner-centered schools. Thinking about schools as brains (rather than machines) and describing them as holographic (rather than two-dimensional) (Morgan, 1997) are useful metaphors for learner-centered schools.

These new metaphors for schooling fit with our core values and our view of a "good-enough vision" to guide system transformation for all students. Many schools have developed vision statements that describe an ideal future, and they have posted these vision statements far and wide on the school's walls, letterhead, and Web site for all to see. This notion of a vision leads school people to believe that their vision of excellence is attainable, that they can reach that point when their ideals are frozen in time and things are just perfect. When the vision does not become reality or when they do not make sufficient progress, they become disaffected. Skeptics see the visioning process as farcical because they do not believe having a vision of an improved future helps. Because the vision is couched in the language of perfection, few believe that it can become a reality.

In our view, schools need to develop a good-enough vision that sets forth their ideals and purposes in practical language that is widely understood and disseminated. Embedded in the idea of a good-enough vision is the notion that the vision develops and evolves as times and contexts change. The vision they develop has to be "good enough" for now. As circumstances change and improve, it is regularly revisited, discussed, wrestled with, and reoriented. The vision is a dynamic, continuously evolving shared understanding about the school and its purposes and values. It is not good enough in the sense that it settles for anything less than excellence for all students. But it is good enough to let the school get started on realizing what the school and all its constituents can become. In the remainder of this chapter, we describe some elements of a good-enough vision and provide some guidance and stories that leaders can use as they work to transform their schools.

Build the Whole Into All the Parts

According to Morgan (1997) and Sergiovanni (1996), binding the school community to core values, purposes, and vision provides the chief means to help all participants understand and enroll in efforts to meet the challenges of the whole enterprise. "Just as DNA in nature carries a holographic code that contains the information required to unfold the complete development of the human body, it is possible to encode key elements of a 'complete organization' in the cultural and other codes that unite its members" (Morgan, 1997, p. 102). Organization members must understand the purposes and central principles that guide the organization before they can successfully intervene in the organization's actions. Rather than requiring compliance with organizational mandates, leaders should seek enrollment in the organization's purposes.

Enrollment in the core values and vision of an organization requires extensive dialogue and deliberation. For Senge (1990), enrollment is a process of becoming part of something by choice. To be committed to an organization is "a state of being not only enrolled but feeling fully responsible for making the vision happen" (p. 218). Compliance is often confused with commitment because compliance has prevailed for so long, especially in parenting. Senge's contrast between compliance and enrollment (shown in Table 3.1) is instructive for leaders as they gauge who is enrolled in the vision and who is malingering or resisting the vision.

In schools and districts, creating commitment means that leaders at the district and school site must seize those aspects of their current context to begin to converse with community stakeholders about learner-centered principles. The context may be a history of low or high performance. Most often, a large number of students who do not achieve to high standards trigger a discussion about school performance. However, the schools might also be characterized by student boredom of even the top-performing students. Communities see students who come to school either because the law or their parents tell them they have to and another group that is uninspired by what happens at school. When the school's performance is in decline, the educational fate of these students becomes a matter of concern. Leadership in the schools—from the superintendent to principals and teachers—forms the core group of emissaries to enlist others teachers and parents into a dialogue about the purposes of schooling and the kinds of education the communities want for its young people.

Senge (1990) suggests that balancing advocacy and inquiry and knowing when to use dialogue rather than discussion are keys to opening conversations and deliberations about change. School leaders invite participants to inquire about the need for change and what a learner-centered discourse means as a mental model for schooling. Core values and the vision of schooling are the focal point of the inquiry that searches for shared meanings about schooling. Dialoguing is the sense-making opportunity for groups of diverse people to go beyond individual thought to create a pool of common meaning that cannot be surfaced individually. Group members inquiring about complex issues from multiple points of view must suspend their own assumptions in order to listen and consider other

TABLE 3.1
Attitudes Toward the Vision

Commitment	Wants it Will make it happen Creates whatever "laws" (structures) are needed
Enrollment	Wants it Will do whatever can be done within the "spirit of the law"
Genuine compliance	Sees the benefits of the vision Does everything that is expected and more Follows the "letter of the law" Is a "good soldier"
Formal compliance	On the whole, sees the benefit of the vision Does what is expected Is a "pretty good soldier"

Grudging compliance	Does not see the benefits of the vision but
	    does not want to leave
	Does enough of what is expected because
	    he has to
	Lets it be known that he is not really on
	    board

Noncompliance	Does not see the benefits of the vision and will not do what is expected "I won't do it and you can't make me"
Apathy	Neither for nor against the vision No interest, no energy "Is it 5 o'clock yet?"

SOURCE: Senge (1990).

perspectives while sharing their own freely. Dialogue reveals the incoherence of individual thought (Senge, 1990). The collective intelligence of the group leads individuals to understand the complexity of the issues. Prefacing the dialogue with an explanation like this will help leaders orient the group toward dialogical inquiry and commitment:

We are trying to find a common ground that will provide our students and community with a sense of the purpose for education. We are also trying to identify a set of core values that provides a foundation for our practices that encourage high student motivation and responsibility for learning. Finally, we need all participants to suspend their assumptions for a short time so that we can hear one another and try to come to as broad a consensus as possible. In the end, we want a set of core values and a "good-enough vision" that informs how all school community members work collaboratively to support the purposes of education we value for all our youngsters.

Although the district office and board of education might desire unanimity among school constituents, it is more important to create a place to start the community dialogue within schools and the community. Spilliane (1998) reminds us that district office professional associations and connections are often associated with different specializations that promote different theories and approaches to curriculum and instruction. Those differences should be shared and tested by promoting a dialogue on their meaning throughout the schools. Attention to getting everyone on the same page regarding the need for change, while not promoting any single approach, encourages divergent thinking and alternative approaches to meeting the challenges the schools face.

We have learned from observing our leadership colleagues across the nation that core values and a good-enough vision often never spread beyond those participants who originally constructed the guiding statements. The opportunity to create a unity of purpose, which was often intended by strategic planners, is often never repeated. As a result, most staff and many other community constituents fail to get on board to validate or confirm a sense of purpose. If they missed out or were not prepared to participate in the initial wave of the dialogue, they were left out. If they have not voiced their concerns about adopting new ways of thinking about learning and its consequences for student accountability, it is easy to understand their ambivalence and resistance to enrollment. Fullan (1998) reminds us that there will be people who are silent and that should not be interpreted as a sign of commitment or agreement. Leadership must seek out the silent and learn from their concerns. He writes, "In turbulent times the key task of leadership is not to arrive

at early consensus, but to create opportunities for learning from dissonance. Mobilizing people to tackle tough problems is the key skill
needed these days" (p. 8). Leadership should strive to get waves of
participants on board each year by allowing frequent return to the
dialogue surrounding the need for change.

Building the whole into the parts also requires networked intelligence. All members of the school-community must have the opportunity to participate in an evolving system of organizational development that develops collective memory and intelligence. In
schools, this dimension of implementation begins with the core values of collaboration and new ways of defining the work of teachers
and students. School people must extend the core values into the
heart of the learning process and assess student perceptions of how
they are progressing toward each other.

Minimum Critical Specifications to
Fulfill the "Good-Enough Vision"

Agents in complex adaptive systems need both the freedom and
the capacity to evolve (Morgan, 1997). Each school in a district needs
the freedom to self-organize and the autonomy to experiment with
its own personal and organizational resources. In many businesses
as well as schools, central management has a tendency to overdefine
and overprescribe what is critical to attend to in implementation.
Morgan (1997) argues that the rule for central management is to
define only what is absolutely essential, and then allow each school,
department, project group, program area, or teacher to launch the
initiative without further specification. In Morgan's terms, central
office management needs to refrain from being the grand designer
in favor of facilitation, orchestration, and boundary management,
creating enabling conditions that allow the local school to experiment and create its own road map to success. This does not mean the
district administration should create anarchy in the name of decentralization. Fullan (1994) argues that both centralization and decentralization are necessary. Finding the balance between overcen-
tralization and laissez-faire decentralization comes through two
facilitating conditions: a good-enough vision and the minimum critical specifications that a school site must include in its action plans.
We have suggested a set of minimum specifications for individual
units within a school or a school as a planning unit for school-site

TABLE 3.2
Minimum Specifications for School-Site Unification Planning

All students have access to the general education curriculum.

All students are to be served at the local school site unless negotiated individually with their parents and the central office.

All resources generated by these students are to be kept by the school site.

All students are to be assessed by the same district and state standards and methods of assessment unless a substitute curriculum is designated.

TABLE 3.3
Central Office Responsibilities in Support of
Self-Managed Teams at the School-Site Level

Develop enabling policy and processes to support site unification of all supportive services to all students

Develop, secure, and distribute resources to school-site level in support of site-level unification of services

Monitor success and needs of site-level implementation efforts, acknowledge success, and provide incentives for innovation as a part of the district knowledge management system of promising practices

Provide direct support when requested

Maintain and update all legal requirements and prepare state and federal reports

Contract with external agency for services

Serve as a forum for staff, parent, student, and community information on all local services, innovations, and promising practices

---

unification of services in a school (see Table 3.2). Table 3.3 lists central office management support services to schools and the district obligations.

Building a Network to Collect Organizational Intelligence

Creating the culture and climate for organizational learning requires commitment to continuous improvement and self-organization. Organizational learning principles are not a blueprint for organizational learning but, according to Morgan (1997), a cycle of activities that reflect "a mind-set and an approach through which we can mobilize key insights about the holograph qualities of the brain in organizational contexts" (p. 115).

Building network intelligence begins with the student database management system, which must begin with common outcomes and be an individual student-based network system. Teams of teachers have access to individual student goals and performance assessment data tied to the performance standards that individual students are pursuing. The databased system is a key infrastructure dimension to support the new work of schools—building the capacity to respond to variability in student learning—and building a common database of curriculum and instruction. Teachers use this second database to facilitate individual and group learning. Through the data collection system, teachers share their instructional structures and processes with one another.

Standards-based reform provides the common outcomes that influence the need for learning opportunities and instructional strategies that teachers can share across the school district. Teacher teams can choose units of study for development, pilot-test, and share their learning in regular seminars and support their dissemination in the district's Web pages on the Internet. The student management system is the basis of continual improvement and ties teacher improvement to student achievement.

Teacher Work Teams

Morgan (1997) recommends developing organizational structures that intensify and focus, rather than dissipate and scatter, intrinsic motivation to engage in more challenging practices of teaching and learning. He acknowledges the lack of variation in the structure of schools. Most schools hinder the development of professional community because of their size and emphasis on bureaucratic control. Like Joyce and Calhoun (1995) and Meier (1995), Morgan (1997) suggests more variation in structure, including small schools, more schools subdivided into smaller units or cells, and more ways of linking highly motivated teachers with "their less ambitious and reflective colleagues—but not structures that isolate the true believers from the skeptical and timid" (p. 20). In the absence of such structures, "there will be no connective tissue to bind teachers together in a relationship of mutual obligation and force them to sort out issues of practice" (p. 20).

In learner-centered schools, the basic unit of design is the work team—teachers of all types organized into teams that take responsibility for all student learning. Work teams become self-managing work groups responsible for developing individual plans; assessing individual student progress; providing direct instruction; supporting individual student project learning; grouping core teams of students for selected learning opportunities; scheduling; and managing physical space, instructional resources, and time. Collaborative teams of three to seven teachers responsible for 50 to 150 students in multiage and multiyear arrangements are an effective strategy for creating learning opportunities that respond to the needs of all students. If groups of students consist of approximately 10% of students who have disabilities, then approximately one of every three teachers should be an instructional specialist who is trained to individualize instruction for diverse learners. For a highly impacted student population, we would assume the same teacher team configurations with a smaller student population of 40 to 120 students. A team of specialists in music, art, computer graphics, and health (or physical education) serves as another work team that supports student learning in the arts for part of the school day. One arts-oriented team per school of 600 students is a good ratio to consider.

Each team member is a multiskilled generalist who is able to perform the instructional tasks needed to assist all students in acquiring proficiency toward meeting standards. Teams meet daily to plan and make decisions regarding programs for their core groups of students. They also manage their communication to parents, plan group learning opportunities within their thematic units, and develop demonstration opportunities and days for students to share their work with their parents and other core groups when appropriate. Each operating team has a designated leader "who acts as a resource, coach, and facilitator and who has a special concern for the team's identity" (Morgan, 1997, p. 106). The team leader represents the team on the school council, which plans schoolwide events, problem-solves, shares successes and needs, and negotiates time and resources.

Morgan (1997) also argues that these work teams start to absorb the functions played by other administrators and departments in more bureaucratic organizations. "There seems to be a natural tendency to 'embrace the whole' in the sense that teams are responsible and rewarded for effective performance of a set of tasks. As soon as these work teams start to realize it, work becomes a lot easier and more effective if they are able to influence and shape the context and conditions effecting their performance" (p. 107). Teacher teams may require some specialized support from outside their ranks.

In closing this discussion, two additional points need to be made. First, all teams of teachers need to be supported to find their pathways to implement the core values and vision. As they face challenges, their school-site leadership teams and the district school transformation council need to provide timely assistance. Second, each year this district council needs to examine results and align them with the means that each team has used to determine if new standards of performance need to be added to or revised. These standards may relate to new student outcomes, instructional processes and learning units, management and communication systems, and quality indicators or rubrics to measure student performance in new ways.

Building on Redundancy

Redundancy is the excess capacity in an organization that can create innovation and organizational development. Individual organizational units are the nodes on the network of intelligence that can encourage initiatives from multiple sources. If each unit is seen as an incubator of ideas, this process can generate multiple, competing "drafts" of intelligence (Morgan, 1997). Of particular importance to our discussion of redundancy in schools is Morgan's description of the redundancy of parts and functions. Redundancy of parts occurs

- When each part is designed to perform a specific function (speech or language personnel to oral communication needs of students)

- When special parts are added to the system for purposes of control (psychologists to assess for student eligibility for special services)
- When replacement parts (specialized teachers by disability certification for identified students) are used to supplant other working parts in the organization (regular class teachers)

Redundancy of parts occurs frequently in schools that are organized as professional bureaucracies. Specialization and compartmentalization of the educational process are examples of redundancy of parts-thinking in schools. Adding special educators who have been trained to work with students with specific disabilities and separating those students and teachers into special classes and resource rooms result from understanding teachers, teaching, and students in terms of redundancy of parts.

Redundancy of functions occurs when functions are added to operating parts rather than providing additional parts. Each part performs a broad range of functions, and team members acquire more skills so that they can substitute for one another. Redundancy of functions occurs in schools when teachers co-teach and share responsibility for the performance of all students in the classroom. These redundancies are critical to self-organizing units of teachers as they become more able to problem-solve and organize learning across the outcomes desired for all students. According to Morgan (1997),

holograph design encourages people to get involved in the challenges at hand, whatever they may be and wherever they come from, rather than focusing on narrow job descriptions and adopting the "that's not my responsibility" attitude typical of more mechanistic approaches to "the management of the practice." (p. 111)

Using Time

Schools generally do not provide the time for teachers to develop their ideas with one another, nor do they provide the capacity-building activities necessary to develop teachers' abilities to think, learn, and collaborate effectively. Elmore (1996) argues that structures that promote learning new practices and incentive systems that support them are often lacking. Starting prototypes that figure out their own road map for making the good-enough vision a reality for themselves and their students has proven to be an effective strategy for supporting teacher development. Teachers learn new, complex practices most successfully through direct observation of their peers, trial and error learning in their classrooms, and regular opportunities to reflect on their implementation with expert practitioners.

We have been fortunate to work with schools that have been successful at creating innovation in teacher development. In Clark County, Indiana, Director of Special Education Ann Schnepf has been developing in-school structures for teams of teachers to plan for the inclusion of students with special needs. These teams have been supported to plan their own model of practice and identify exemplary sites to visit, consultants to bring in, and their own on-off site training. Their plan must be accepted by the schoolwide committee on program improvement. Teachers receive $25 per hour for up to 15 hours per year as sanctioned by the school plan. Marilyn Friend and William Bursuch (1996) has argued that co-teaching is a significant factor in both student and teacher learning. Through co-teaching, teachers have an in-class professional development model to emulate, reflect with, and provide feedback about their teaching.

To support in-school release time, a high school team of four administrators and two counselors was used to free up teachers for a half day each quarter to facilitate their collaborative planning and co-teaching of math, English, history, and health. In another school district, any teacher team ready to build its own prototypic response to the district's good-enough vision or to replicate another team's model is provided a weeklong intensive workshop annually. Beginning in January, the team begins planning one day each month with an in-school teacher or administrator facilitator. A week of summer planning time is also provided.

Requisite Variety

Since it is nearly impossible to give everyone all the information and skills they need for every possible situation in the school environment, Morgan (1997) recommends "building multifunctional teams. These teams collectively possess the requisite skills and abilities, where each individual member is as generalized as possible, creating a pattern of overlapping skills and knowledge bases in the team over-all" (p. 113). Morgan contends that teams do not survive and evolve if they do not recognize the changes in their clients, their needs, or their environments. Evolution and adaptability of teams are more likely to occur, if redundancy of function and requisite variety are built in at the point of interaction with the client and the environment. Structures need to be developed in a cellular manner around self-organizing, multidisciplinary teams that have the requisite skills and abilities to deal with the diversity of the student body in a holistic and integrated way (Elmore, 1996). This means reaching out to all staff to bring their considerable talents to the team table and create the learning opportunities students need to reach the mutual goals we have negotiated with them.

This lesson is especially visible in special education programs where regional cooperatives had most of the responsibility and all the expertise about educating students with special needs. These cooperatives operated at a distance from local schools and teachers. Innovation was more likely to come from the cooperative rather than the local school because the local school was not obligated to respond to the needs of the students. Local capacity was diminished, responsibility was displaced, and students with special needs were relegated to the bottom of the learning progress charts.

Reculturing Schools
to Become Learner-Centered

Fullan (1993, 1998) has called for reculturing, rather than restructuring, schools. Reculturing "involves changing the norms, values, incentives, skills, and relationships in the organization to foster different ways of working together" (1993, p. 9) to affect teaching and learning. Restructuring was primarily structural, and school organization was focused. In 1998, Fullan argued that reculturing is largely a call to leadership to seek an emotional connection between people. Change agents must cope with the pressure to maintain the current reality of schools as they pursue the second-order changes that would transform them. The more complex the change, the less it can be forced. During the period of prototyping and developing unique pathways, problems are friends that change agents must encounter in order to learn. Individual entrepreneurialism and collective efforts are necessary for balanced growth. Decentralization and centralization strategies must be employed simultaneously for implementation to be successful.

Fullan (1998) also reminds school and district leaders that they must manage emotionally as well as rationally. What is needed is to instill and sustain hope in the teaching staff. Daily, teachers and administrators risk substituting old beliefs for new ones while taking on new ventures that reek of uncertainty. Although they may understand that hope is not a promise, teachers will need "to be reminded that they are connected to a larger purpose and to others who are struggling to make progress" (p. 10).

What we now envision is what Joyce and Calhoun (1995) call a "quantum leap toward the creation of a setting where inquiry is normal and the conditions of the workplace support continuous, collegial inquiry" (p. 51). School reinvention and renewal are inquiry processes, not recipes or formulas. Burrello, Tracy, and Schultz (1973) have written that, when special education acts as experimental education, it helps members of the host system understand how certain groups of students learn. Specialized personnel collaborate with their colleagues in the host system to provide those conditions necessary for students with special needs to be successful in the regular classrooms. What we have learned is that there is no "host system." Children deserve to be thought of as individuals, regardless of their circumstances. Separating them from one another by some arbitrary set of characteristics is unfair and ineffective. Our new-millennium society needs all children to contribute economically and socially. Education should be special for any student. As we learn how to personalize education for all students, that just may come true.

4

Incentives as Attractors

Why Things Remain the Same and
How to Change Them

Over the past two decades we have had the opportunity to look through the windows of several school districts across the nation. Our work has entailed responding to leaderships' requests to evaluate the effectiveness of their special education programs and to provide professional development that prepares school personnel for change in programs for students with disabilities. Even though leaders often know, or think they know, the right thing to do, they recognize the difficulty and complexity of moving a critical mass of others to do the right thing.

We think the concept of incentives—those of individuals, coalitions, collectives or groups and those of the broader systems impinging on education and their effect on one another—is a useful tool for facilitating change. Incentives are motives either to do something or to resist doing it; they are *attractors* in the complex adaptive-systems sense. Attraction and resistance impact on one another to create a dynamic system of incentives that can keep things the same or change the way we work. Systems tend toward equilibrium. When they fall into a state of disequilibrium—when they are out of balance and unstable—the incentives that are proposed to restore the status quo or to create a new equilibrium are crucial to enrolling the organization's people in efforts to change. The incentive exchanges that are negotiated substitute a desirable motivating factor (which encourages change) for another equally satisfying factor (which encourages a return to an unchanged state of stability).

If we believe that those things that matter in an organization cannot be decreed from on high (Fullen, 1993), then we must learn to read the organization and access the levers that affect how and why people in organizations do what they do. The context in which this analysis takes place is an organic system of embedded relationships. Discussions of moral purpose, the rights of students with disabilities, and poor postschool outcomes alone are not enough to change internal and external stakeholders' beliefs about what works in teaching and learning for students with special needs. We must study, write, talk, and teach about how to leverage real changes in practice in educational systems.

Darling-Hammond (1997) has written about incentives as opportunities for ownership, invention, and support for teachers to pursue individual interests. The public assessment process in itself becomes an incentive because it establishes standards and recognizes the students' status relative to them. Darling-Hammond also identifies incentives for students, including standards and supports for learning, autonomy, participation, choice, and the home-school connection that a learner-centered school approach promotes.

In the remainder of this chapter, we provide five case studies in an effort to offer an analysis of what keeps people practicing in the same bureaucratic and political way in spite of both evidence and stakeholders who hold countervailing views to the contrary. A tabular representation of these case studies is provided in Resource A. We examine the contexts, issues, disequilibrium, and incentive exchanges that occurred in these districts to offer some insights into how attractors—incentives and resistors—come into play to maintain organizations and to encourage them to change.

An Eastern Seaboard District:
A Case of Inertia

The Context

The director of special education in this district had been in place for more than 25 years. He had more tenure in the central office than any other individual, including the superintendent. He was less than 5 years away from retirement when we began our program evaluation study. The director had built the classic special education empire. Each year, more students, and with them many more dollars, flowed from the general system into his domain. At that time, 20% of the students were identified as having disabilities, and a corresponding 20% of the district's $25 million budget was spent on students with disabilities. More and more of the budget bought him more staff and more of the district's discretionary power. Most students with any significant behavioral involvement were sent out of the district as were most students with multiple and severe disabilities.

The director paid selective attention to the various audiences who needed access to him, and he wore the enormous number of pink phone slips he received as a badge of honor in his daily battle to protect the district's resources and program integrity. He protected *his* teachers and staff under the guise of compliance with state and federal regulations. Why should he want to turn the system upside down now?

The teacher's union was concerned about working conditions. It had successfully negotiated and maintained a policy of weighting special needs students, thus keeping integrated class sizes small and improving working conditions for general and special education personnel. Teachers' rights, rather than sound educational practice, drove district decision making. Adults were at the center of this system; students were not.

Special educators were unwittingly supporting the working conditions priority of the union that enable it to get students who could not make it in the mainstream out of the regular class. The only attempt at collaboration was teacher centered and workload related. Two teachers were scheduled in the high schools to serve 12 to 15 special education students in English and math with a subject-oriented teacher and a special education teacher. This program merely reduced the subject matter teacher's load. There was no evidence of higher levels of student performance or even an attempt at social integration of students with special learning needs. Principals openly questioned and lobbied against this practice because it reduced their flexibility to schedule general education staff and it also created an inequity in personnel loads for both types of staff.

On the surface, it would seem that these two entities, the director (and his programs) and the union (and its teachers) are adversaries. The director's incentives are related to regulatory compliance and keeping costs affordable. The union's incentives are focused on maximizing teacher discretion and financial advantage. But they have negotiated a mutually satisfactory equilibrium. Their incentives, which are generally perceived to be at odds, are in perfect harmony. They do not see themselves as resisting change. Instead, they see themselves as protecting the integrity of the classroom for most students and providing nurturing, needs-responsive resource rooms and special class supports for students with disabilities. Keeping things the way they are preserves their vision of what should be.

In this district, parents are by and large uninformed. Professionals tell them what is best for their children. What is best is a highly specialized, individualized, separate, and often private educational program. Recently, however, a bright, knowledgeable family (he, an Ivy League professor and she, a professional child advocate), whose teenager has developmental disabilities, decided to challenge the district's practice of separate but equal special programming. A hearing occurred and sparks flew. The teenager is now able to attend typical high school classes with excellent integration opportunities—a program designed by his parents. But nothing has changed for the other students his age with disabilities. The challenging parents resisted the status quo and caused some friction, but they got the desired change for their child. In the process, the district received access to resources in the form of national experts who attested to the appropriateness of the parents' recommended practice for similarly situated students. But the incentives are so established to resist change that the change can occur only one student at a time. In effect, the director and the district are saying "You want change? Sue us! We like what we have. It works for us. If you want things different, you'll have to take a risk to get it."

Disequilibrium

In addition to a few parents asking questions and seeking individualized programming, the director of special education also had to deal with other central office administrators, who had been perfectly content to have students with disabilities off their plates. They have benefited from the practice of placing special needs students out of sight into resource rooms, separate classes, and even private day programs. The convenience of not having to deal with hard-to-teach students allowed them to ignore the dollars flowing into the special education subsystem at disproportionate rates. Again, the administrators who competed for resources had negotiated an equilibrium in which the special education program kept student failure out of sight (and out of mind) in return for a substantial share of the budget.

The district's budget is reviewed and approved by city government. During a recent round of budget negotiations, the mayor raised questions and requested that the school board bring in a group of commercial auditors to assess the special education program and its costs. The feedback from the auditors' recommendations was so negative that the director of special education and the superintendent contracted with us to conduct our study.

The superintendent described the special education program as a sieve. We thought it was more like a faucet. He indicated that the special education leadership often presented him with mutually exclusive options—either serve a child in the private day school or the district is out of compliance. When parents requested inclusive settings, the district offered what they had—special classes or resource rooms. The director defended the system in terms of compliance—a continuum of services was required and was in place. The superintendent was being held hostage by his subordinate in special education.

In addition to the problem of current high costs, the director argued that he was unable to file a budget with any confidence because of the unpredictability of student needs and the services they might require. In each of the past 4 years, the special education budget increased from $100,000 to $300,000 over the course of a year because new students with disabilities were identified or moved to the district and their services had not been accounted for in the budget process. The unpredictability of special education enrollments throughout the year created a great deal of havoc for the board and its reporting to the city government.

The power of the director of special education and his itinerant emissaries—psychologists, speech-and-hearing specialists, social workers, and special education resource teachers—resided in their specialized expertise. Their responsibility was to identify and place students: to get them out of the mainstream. Once placed, the students became the responsibility of the special education subsystem—not general education teachers, counselors, and principals—to provide an appropriate education. The incentives were the specialized expertise and gatekeeping role, which gave both staff and administrator unequal status. The bigger the program, the larger the staff and budget the director controlled and the more he was able to dole out favors and perks to selected staff and schools.

The negotiated equilibrium that existed in this school district became unstable when attention and political pressure were brought to bear on the system by external constituencies. Costs, the lack of equity across services and school sites, the principal's concerns about parity among staff, the lack of special education personnel's expectations for student success, parental complaints about the slowness of the referral and placement processes, the lack of inclusionary placements, and the lack of in-district options brought the system into disequilibrium.

Incentives Exchange

While the study findings were being drafted, the director went on medical leave for a year and expressed his intent to resign. The district began to search for a new set of incentives that might change the nature of the service delivery model and help create the momentum for change. Although the district was technically in compliance with the continuum of services provision of IDEA, it was out of compliance with the law's intent for maximum feasible participation of students with disabilities in the least restrictive environment. The district had few provisions for student participation in the general education curriculum and assessment of student progress in the state assessment process.

A public information campaign for internal and external stakeholders was proposed to provide a vehicle for examining current practice and identifying incentives to search for alternatives. For parents, a fresh and long-overdue review of their rights and new roles in assessment and placement decisions could heighten their interest and commitment to participate more fully in their child's educational planning. The campaign could include a review of case law to confront the union and its position on the teacher's role in the implementation of the general education curriculum. The incentive in the public information campaign was the desire to remain in compliance with the law and to avoid expensive and adversarial lawsuits.

The district had two recent examples of successful inclusion of severely disabled students that it could build on through extensive inservice and in-class support for teachers. The district had willing principals with special education expertise who could be partners in building in-school programs for out-of-district students. Principals also knew that they would get a significant proportion of the resources that these students generated. The incentive to program locally attracted principals to the idea of locating special education programs in their schools, when the funding for out-of-district placements followed the child.

Because the district's student population was changing and curriculum reform was budding to meet the needs of a more vulnerable population of students, the use of resource teachers as in-class supports to regular teachers provided an excellent means to develop in-service training about adapting and individualizing instruction for more students. Historically, special education had not comingled its comprehensive system of personnel development funds or co-trained any general education staff. Those dollars were controlled and used exclusively by special educators. The needs of the students and the lack of teacher expertise to deal with diverse students coalesced to create an attractor that would increase teacher competence and efficacy in dealing with needy students.

The parents as well as the principals wanted more equity across schools. Though most students were already in their home schools, there were a few notable exceptions. Parents would be a key ally in raising the level of district awareness about the need to treat all students more alike than differently. Parents needed to be invited into the budget process and learn to speak for the needs of the schools in their changing communities. Parents simply did not know how to advocate for the public schools within city government.

Some of these parents held a vision of what might be that was truly inspiring. Many of them could become advocates for change along with those staff members who also held a different vision for students with disabilities in the district. Creating the moral purpose for the education of students with disabilities in this community was an important and necessary first step in the change process.

A New England District:
A Case of Friction

The Context

This district was filled with multiple best practices for all students. Its weakest links were its programs for students with severe disabilities and a special education support staff that could not always justify its practices. When the principal of this elementary district came to the school in 1991, she was pleased to see that all the individual elements of best practice in multiage classrooms, active and cooperative learning, and a strong commitment to personalizing education for every student were in place. The school board supported innovation in programming, school structure, teaming, and technology. Some teachers were also committed to the mission of personalized education and they were pioneering new learner-centered principles of learning and instruction. Students were actively planning and determining their weekly lessons under the tutelage of their teachers. Every child had an individual, 25-page plan to outline a course of study. Rubrics were developed by the students to communicate their progress through the individual student plan. But all was not well.

Disequilibrium

The friction resulted from five factors, three related to community and parent concerns and two to the majority of the teaching staff. Parents were unsure of what was expected of their children in school and were concerned about whether their children were learning what their cousins in Shaker Heights, Ohio, or Shawnee Mission, Kansas, were learning. Some parents were concerned that their children were given too much responsibility for their own learning and that teachers were abdicating their responsibility for deciding what and how students must learn. The teaching staff believed that at least two thirds of the students were not motivated to be in school. They were not satisfied with only teaching to the one third who came prepared to be led by the teacher. Teachers also felt that they needed to make their teaching more inquiry oriented to facilitate the development of critical thinking and problem-solving skills that they and the community valued. Too much teaching of science, for example, consisted of studying those who did the science. They wanted their students to do the science themselves and embraced a project-learning approach to all content areas.

Incentives Exchange

During the period 1991 through 1995, the principal repeatedly took surveys of parents to assess how the staff was responding to concerns for clarity of the curriculum and the desired student outcomes, as well as how those outcomes were assessed. The principal saw the state standards-based reform movement as a means to solve the problem of her school's selection of unique outcomes. The state standards movement provided the incentive for students, teachers, and parents to adopt a common language about outcomes. The net effect of the standards movement was that the school could not be held up as an experimental school with a unique curriculum that was unrecognizable in neighboring school districts or states.

The state standards-based reform also complemented the self-referenced assessment model used in the school with the state's norm referenced test. The principal worked hard to get the staff comfortable with both types of assessments. She was concerned that the teachers did not know how to assess what they valued in terms of student outcomes. With data they collected over the 3 years, they showed that the school well outranks its neighbors and that selected houses or families within the school show superior results. These data have silenced the earlier parent critics who complained about student empowerment and its influence on student achievement.

Staff concerns with the transformation of the school from teacher-centered to learner-centered were primarily related to their participation in determining the mission and its meaning for their practice. The principal wisely spent the better part of her first year gaining teacher enrollment in the board's vision and mission. She also provided ongoing support for new teacher teams to redesign their practice to become more thematic and interdisciplinary and to broaden their 2-year multiage teams into 4-year teams. The fact that the school was developing in-house models of the new work of students and teacher practice facilitated the spread of the innovation.

Other incentives included summer in-service; planning time with a teacher or administrator mentor starting in January; and additional technology, including a data management system that teachers and students used to record their assessments and observations to track student progress. The addition of a classroom assistant to help manage the individualization of student programs was also used as an incentive to teams of teachers.

All students with disabilities in this elementary district were served within the two schools in the district. All students were placed in the schoolhouses and served by the house core team. Teachers and aides supported by special education funds provided their services in the context of the classroom. Only about 50 students were identified and placed during the years 1991 to 1996. Sixteen students with severe disabilities had one-on-one aides.

Over the last few years, more students were identified because the principal and the special education team leader could not find a way to justify staff levels in a totally integrated environment where every child was supported through a personalized plan. The principal created friction over costs of staff for identified students. Her concern was that any intervention counted. Data were not being generated to support interventions that were suggested. Her solution to justify the staffing pattern to the local school board was for more students to be officially identified.

What we learned from this example of a school in transformation is that somebody is asking some hard questions to which no one wants to share the answers. What folks have learned, however, is that the last thing certain people want is for someone to come in and blow their cover. One must uncover the incentives exchange at work to move ahead toward resolving a problem. In this example, in spite of the all the support for change in the school, it did not mean everyone was included. Everyone did not join the change in the first year. Not everyone was willing to admit that they did not know how to make the transformation. Leadership needed the time and patience to develop commitment and enrollment of staff and other stakeholders. Their resistance had to be respected until they could come to believe that the alternative is both better and possible. What this example illustrates is that true believers are made—not converted on faith alone. Self-examination and hard work are necessary for teachers to transform themselves from solo practitioners to team players who share resources and learn together.

This principal used the concept of self-organization from complex adaptive-systems thinking to facilitate multiple pathways to more learner-centered teams. There was never just one way to make it happen. She let teachers and the community know that professionalism was respected, and she challenged everyone to get better. Her leadership and encouragement were ultimately the best incentives to become better. Her leadership message was "Your expectations for yourself are more important than my expectations for you!"

A Midwestern School District: A Case of Momentum

The Context

This suburban district neighbors a major urban center. It enjoys a progressive image and an openness to diversity. Its budget grew throughout the 1990s with the growth of students because of the state's generous growth formula. It has had a successful busing program in its schools from the urban district. Its special needs program has always been a state leader in inclusive elementary settings. Its director was one of the first to include all students with mild disabilities in the state's high stakes testing program. Twenty-five percent of the eligible students passed the test on the first round and another 27% in the second. The district's high schools enjoy an excellent academic reputation.

Disequilibrium

With a new court order that is ending one-way busing and the end of the growth cycle, the district's annual budget took a major hit and all units of the district were asked to examine their programs and reduce their budgets significantly. Special services employs a case manager model. A teacher might have a case load of 50 students and 5 to 10 instructional aides. The aides provide the in-class support for most students with mild disabilities. The special education staff handles all the case management responsibilities, plans the individual programs with general education teachers and aides, and supports the aides in the implementation of the program. The director is faced with two challenges in maintaining the current case management model. The cost of aides with their benefit package rivals a first-year teacher's salary, and the quality of available aides has been declining as teacher shortages in the state have grown. Other more financially rewarding opportunities in a robust economy have led to fewer and fewer quality people available for these entry-level positions.

Because of the pending budget crunch, both the director and individual principals are concerned that parents and teachers alike will join forces and resist any change in the case management model. The director fears due process hearings from parents, and the principals fear that teachers will refuse to accept instructional responsibility for students with disabilities unless aide support is provided in their classrooms. The district's exemplary inclusion model is threatened.

Incentives Exchange

The incentive for parents and teachers to keep things as they are is the in-class one-on-one support the aide provides the identified students. For parents seeking extra help and support for their child's learning needs, it is important that the teacher have additional help to provide the needed instructional support to adapt the curriculum or instruction.

The district leadership is aware that the student body is growing more diverse and needy in this highly academically oriented school district. The incentive that the principals, director, and assistant superintendent have been discussing is the move to more self-organization and the appeal to teacher professionalism in finding a way to share their well-developed human resources more effectively. Self-organization appeals to teachers to think outside their own boundaries, schedules, and use of resources. Rather than grade-level teams with teachers retaining an individual age cohort for a single year, the teachers could be asked to consider multiage arrangements and more flexible scheduling within a house concept that includes special education teachers who provide appropriate instruction for all students. Challenging teacher teams to develop more personalized educational plans for all students is the key to getting students to take more responsibility for their own learning. The chief incentives for teachers are having more time together to plan as a collegial teaching team and using the resident expertise available on a full-time basis to adapt and modify curriculum and instruction.

The director thinks that hiring additional teachers—rather than continuing to increase the number of instructional aides—may be an incentive for parents. His focus is that adding expertise and collaboration will lead to a better learning environment in the general education classroom for included students. Other incentives are the availability of more sophisticated computer instructional software to support individualized student learning and the increased use of project learning in the curriculum. Inviting students to take more responsibility for their own learning requires learning settings that students can use independently or with minimum teacher support. The computer-authoring programs provide an excellent vehicle for peer learning. Finally, computer technology is an excellent means for students to be perceived as expert and for them to take on teaching responsibilities for other students.

A related incentive is a computer management program that supports teachers and students. The computer program provides the infrastructure to support (a) developing, recording, and printing personal student plans aligned with state standards; (b) the framework to guide the student's weekly implementation plan and teacher-student conferencing to increase student on-task behavior, monitor progress, and motivate through teacher and peer feedback; (c) a means to record and tally student and teacher assessment of student progress; and (d) a means to create a longitudinal record and report card to parents and school officials monitoring student performance.

Another incentive is the competition as well as the cooperation between teams to find solutions to serving all students more appropriately. Identifying and promoting team success within the school, the district, and the state by sharing ideas that work, providing co-training, and promoting conferencing around their ideas with others acknowledges team learning and compliments the staff on a job well done.

The last incentive is continuing opportunities to reflect with others and support continuous improvement. Networking with universities and other school districts within the state and region is another follow-up activity for district leadership to support and acknowledge the learning demonstrated by staff. Contributing to the standards of the teaching practice in the community is the key outcome for the district leadership as well as the individual school staff.

A Northeastern Urban District: Another Case of Inertia

The Context

Unlike the eastern seaboard district, this district has active central office leadership and support from school-site principals. Special education, Title I, and English as a second language staff all blend their services at the school site under the leadership of the site administrator. The director also enjoys solid community support and actively involves the community in budget planning and program development. A knowledgeable and socially conscious community makes acceptance of disability a significant factor in this district's programming success. Yet the director sensed a case of inertia. Staff were more content and satisfied than not. Most observers thought the dissatisfaction was ambiguous, transitory, and situational.

The director believed that her staff were struggling with inclusion and the increasing case management responsibilities that state and federal regulations bring. She felt that the district needed a push out of its state of inertia. Her staff were competent in assessment, case management, and rule compliance, but they complained of role erosion. Less and less of their time was being spent in actual instruction. They spent their time planning student programs and sharing them with general education teachers and instructional aides.

The district leadership promoted a strategic plan for the district and was actively collecting district and state normative assessment data to demonstrate student progress to its public. The district has the state's highest poverty rate, and affected schools were falling further and further behind. The strategic plan was also being used to guide special education goal setting and report student progress.

Disequilibrium

The district director of special education requested an external program evaluation to assess the state of the district's evolution toward contemporary standards of practice. She pinpointed specific school-level issues at selected elementary schools, one middle school, and the high school.

The director read the need for a district tune-up quite well. A district with an excellent reputation for special services had stopped questioning and critically examining its practice at the staff level. The district also had a new superintendent (less than 3 years in the job) and a number of principal retirements and new assignments (about one third of its schools), which provided an opportunity to reexamine program practices. Finally, an external budget committee had asked the director to consider a set of questions it had about middle school and the high school special education programs and personnel assignments.

Incentives Exchange

The primary incentive for conducting the program evaluation study of the district's programs in special services was a validation of the director's own perceptions of her services and the need to create a future agenda with her colleagues centrally and at individual school sites. The fact that she enjoyed almost universal support and that she alone knew the history of the district advantaged her in negotiations with her superiors, peers, and staff. Her external audiences and new principal leadership in many schools were also raising questions that she needed to investigate. Since she was planning to retire in the next 5 years, she was starting to think about her legacy and maintaining the district's special services reputation.

In the program evaluation, we came to understand and validate a number of the things the director agreed with and questioned. She and the evaluation team discussed how best to encourage staff and schools to begin to change from their comfortable status quo to a new vision of special services in the district. In subsequent dialogue with her and the district assistant superintendent for curriculum and assessment, we outlined a number of possible new incentives to consider to set out her future agenda.

Because the district had an existing norm of site-based decision making and the director was comfortable with the history of sites' assuming responsibility for special services, we searched for additional incentives to move the staff and school-based leadership forward. We deduced that the director within the umbrella of the district's strategic plan needed to provide "a good-enough vision of what might be." We discerned that school sites lacked a sense of direction. Staff members were caught up in their current practice and in maintaining the processes of identification, assessment, and planning of instruction and services. The quality and extent of involvement of general education personnel in those processes appeared to be limited and instruction was superficial. Special services staff were suffering from role erosion and a high level of ambiguity regarding how to allocate their time responding to multiple requests from students, faculty, and parents in the district.

The incentive for change was role clarity within a revised mission and vision of special services. Using the school norm of site-based decision making and self-organization, school teams needed a good-enough vision to restart their dialogue about all students within a unified systems perspective and to reinvent themselves and their roles. Appealing to the principal's and staff's sense of professionalism, a good-enough vision gave the staff the impetus to find the time to plan and use the freedom to create new ways of collaboration.

This director had a reservoir of goodwill and trusting relationships with all stakeholders. These decentralized school sites needed a reason to change and to inquire about ways to improve their practice. In addition to the program evaluation report itself, new IDEA and Title I requirements, measures of personnel effectiveness, dissatisfaction with student performance, and their own role needs overshadowed the current context of contentment and reasons to change. The district needed to move from its individual caretaker metaphor for teaching and learning to a more active and collaborative metaphor.

The reputation of the district and the high esteem in which the staff were held by the community also served as incentives. Knowledgeable people in the community knew that the need for change was imminent. A combined task force of community members and the building of a level leadership from the principals and teachers signaled the need for a new set of standards by which school-site teams could measure the discrepancy between the status quo and where they needed to be. The schools needed a vehicle by which new information flowed into schools. The school staffs needed to examine their shared responsibility for students with disabilities. Developing a set of minimum specifications to move to a continuous improvement model based on student performance indicators was just one of a few specifications that were included in the community task force report.

The state's standards-based reform movement and the district's own strategic plan provided incentives for collaboration between general and special service personnel. Special services and general education staff were using the state and district standards with varying degrees of fidelity and intensity to guide their practice. Holding special service staff accountable for state and district performance standards aligned with the district plan offered an incentive for collaboration and demonstrated the similarity of responsibility of special services instructional staff for those instructional expectations set for all teachers. The incentive for special services personnel was that their roles looked more like what all teachers did, which reduced concerns over fundamental points of contention between general and special education teachers—size and lack of accountability for student performance.

Collaboration and in-class support, rather than the tutorial model of pull-out support to students, led to changes in how students were referred and identified, which reduced the assessment and case management responsibilities of special services personnel. A related incentive resulted when personnel in special services became part of the district's public accountability process. A focus on positive student and teacher work that is related to postschool success was the incentive for all to be recognized for their efforts.

The district has adopted a new information system to help reduce the amount of time teachers have to spend repetitively inputting student data. The need for a data management system tied to the state standards and accountability system became another impetus to support the aims of a unified system and reverse the role erosion that was so time consuming. Reducing the overreliance on instructional aides in teaching and differentiating their roles into a data management function served as an incentive to change the case management aspects of the special services role.

A Southwestern School District:
Another Case of Friction

The Context

This large suburban district was beginning its transformation from an all-white, high-performing district to a multiracial and multiethnic district. Its new superintendent, a former special education administrator sensitive to public perception of all the district's program, immediately called for a study of the special education program and its leadership. He was hired in part because of a group of parents who were completely dissatisfied with the equity of programming between schools and the utter lack of attention to parent due-process concerns. From lengthy identification and evaluation processes to the limited programming options within general and special education programs, the superintendent and board of education were concerned about standards and the district's reputation for high academic performance. A group of new middle- and elementary-school principals wanted more from special education, particularly the ability to manage students with behavioral problems. Special education was a parallel system operating within the confines of a typical school, having its own teachers, parallel curriculum, and schedule. Some of the newer principals saw the need to merge programs and services to meet the needs of all students.

The special education leadership changed during the study. The director who was moved was a former principal who happened to have a special education background. She was well-connected to the former superintendent, who wanted someone to heal the wounds caused by previous litigation threats and deal with other parental concerns. Her rhetoric of pacification and acceptance of parents had run its course. Before the course of the program evaluation was completed, a new director was installed by the superintendent and the board of education.

Disequilibrium

The changing demographics of the district focused the leadership and board of education on all students achieving high expectations regardless of race or ethnicity. The board selected a superintendent who would be responsive to all stakeholder claims on the system, not just the majority and achieving white population. The superintendent came from previous leadership positions in elite and urban school districts in the Midwest. He had worked and developed model programs for students with severe disabilities and had successfully closed special schools. His focus was on quality instruction and measurable results. Delivering the message to the "good old boys" in his district and to those who talked a good game but did not perform was his first priority. The culture of the district, particularly in the middle and high school, treated instruction as a sidebar to athletic, band, and cheerleader competitions. The superintendent's bold plan included everyone and held all staff accountable for student academic and social success.

Incentives Exchange

The leadership team at the central office needed a vision and a set of standards to guide the refocusing of their current efforts and choices. The first incentive they grasped was the need to avoid litigation involving lack of attention to parent and student rights for due process.

The evaluation team was quickly able to build a set of recommendations that the new director (another former principal with high peer acceptance and excellent credentials in special education) could accept. The most obvious recommendation was to build on the high school programming model for students with severe disabilities. This excellent program and its quality staff should be recognized for their community-based training model and their work within the high school to build significant peer relations for these students. Our recommendation was to move a successful model program across the three high schools and initiate them into the middle schools. A second related recommendation was to reconfigure the middle school teams to include students with milder disabilities and include their teachers as part of those teams. The incentives to teachers were to dissolve their separate curriculum and schedules, which underutilized personnel and space. Eliminating the overcrowding and freeing up teachers to provide in-class support was appealing to school principals because they were concerned about adapting curriculum and instruction for the more diverse learners entering their already overcrowded schools.

At the high school level, their success with students with severe disabilities raised the question: Why can't we provide a more inclusive experience for students with milder disabilities? The learning resource rooms were active and busy with students coming and going every hour. The special education teachers were hard pressed to see and support all the students coming through their doors. They had little time to consult with subject-matter teachers and they used their students as messengers to link one group of teachers with the other. The general education teachers had little ownership for supporting these students, and the attempts at in-class collaboration appeared to be one teacher teaching and the other drifting from identified student to identified student. Both sets of teachers were dissatisfied with the individual attempts to support in-class subject-matter teaching.

We proposed that the teachers needed to identify their mutual dissatisfactions and determine if they could find a good-enough vision to link their individual goals into common goals. The incentive here was whether we could find a way to reorganize human resources to use the strengths of both sets of teachers to serve all students more appropriately. We focused on the perspective of all students as a means to illustrate how we must support the individual teacher's sense of responsibility for students. We also emphasized the identification of individual contributions and how each would teach one another, leading to a large repertoire of responses to more diverse student learning needs. Clearly, the incentive to move one's practice from the isolation of individual work settings to joint work settings where the common goal was success for all became the starting point for collaboration. A series of validated inclusive practices become the heart of our recommendations.

At many of the elementary schools, we were again impressed with the paperwork requirements and the case management responsibilities of teachers. We were also concerned about the lack of dialogue about quality instruction. The teachers appreciated the changing student demographics and were starved for new ways of serving students with disabilities. The incentive was the need to reduce their reliance on one-to-one tutorials and begin examining the literature about adapting curriculum and instruction. The message was that both general and special education teachers may need to change and that they could help one another to change how they think about diverse learners, expectations, the teaching process, and evaluation criteria.

Another incentive we spoke to in this program evaluation was the need to reconnect substantively with parents and community advocates who had lost their patience with the old special education director and selected building-based leadership. We included a combined teacher and community task force as part of our evaluation process. We went to them on the very first trip to the district and began to solicit their observations and concerns. They reviewed our recommendations before they went to the board of education and the superintendent's cabinet. From our discussions, one incentive for them was that the community task force of general education teachers and parents would continue to advise the new director. As soon as the new director was brought on board, we began to include her in our deliberations with this working committee.

A third incentive was the parent participation survey we instituted as part of the individual accountability school process. For every meeting parents attended, a survey was taken to assess their perception of the quality of their participation in and satisfaction with the conferences they attended in terms of initial referral, evaluation feedback, and conferences for individual educational planning (IEP), annual reviews, and 3-year evaluations. Particular attention was given to the value staff places on parental input and feedback as well as parent understanding of the data and decisions that were made regarding their child's educational program. These surveys were distributed at the end of each parental interaction and sent to the central office for tabulation. An annual assessment was included in each building principal's review.

Summary

Leadership has been preoccupied with the center, the routine, the tried and true, the typical student. From our perspective, an organization cannot be understood or moved from the center. The center merely suggests where the crowd is, not where it needs to go.

Schools have failed to share individual learning about teaching and learning in any systematic way. There are many reasons—lots of data, how it is sorted, time to reflect on it, the nature of solo practice, a lack of structure for thinking about practice, and time. We think the concepts from complex adaptive systems are the key to unleashing the potential of teachers to recraft their roles from those of individual solo performers to a membership in ensembles. Notion of a good-enough vision, minimum specifications, and self-organization are helpful in understanding teaching and learning differently. But the first step in the movement toward learner-centered schools begins with attractors, the incentives that are available to draw people to the tasks at hand.

As professionals, we have learned that we cannot prescribe for other professionals. We start by offering a compelling incentive that fosters growth based on a desire to get better. And we always try to remember: "You don't have to be sick to get better."

5

The Transformation to Learner-Centered

Educators at the turn of the 21st century are feeling increasing pressure to change the way they view the place of schools in the world. Critics of existing systems of education challenge educators to shake loose from their familiar assumptions about how schooling is organized. The call for transforming schools involves more than popular buzzwords, more than an invitation for tinkering; it is a demand for a fundamental shift of dramatic proportions. For us, the shift is not simply the move to *depublicize* the public schools through the use of vouchers or chartered public or private schools. We are calling for something more fundamental. Educators need to examine, question, and change their assumptions about the nature of personal and organizational learning, access to knowledge, power, control, and order. From the classroom to the statehouse, educational and political leaders at all levels must reexamine the premises they use to organize and support schools.

Concurrent with this general call for transformation is an expression of concern about the manner in which services for students with special needs have evolved into systems that are parallel, separate, and largely unequal in spite of the significant financial resources necessary to support them. The debate in the professional community over the usefulness of these programs and the nature of necessary changes has been intense. Proposed remedies have been advanced in the form of a variety of vaguely understood concepts with confusing names—mainstreaming, integration, the regular education initiative, inclusion, and the least restrictive environment. Both the special needs and general education communities have recognized the necessity for a truly unified system that includes all students—a system that does not rely on classification and separation as prerequisites for securing appropriate educational services and fundamental rights for citizens. A unified system framework assumes an inclusive strategy for educating all students with special needs and places responsibility for their education at the doorstep of the local schoolhouse.

In this chapter, we describe the changes in thinking that will be necessary for a system to evolve in which the education of students with special needs occurs within the context of education for all students. Transforming schools to meet the needs of all students through programs that are equitable and excellent requires changes in the ways we understand schooling, teaching, and learning. We describe the need for a paradigm shift for education and highlight those aspects that have become increasingly important for educators to consider as they reinvent schools. We also explore the development of new mental models that educational leaders can use to harness the power of organizational learning and professional development in their schools. We then explore emerging practices and discourses about the restructuring of public education and identify their implications for students with disabilities and special needs and for special support personnel. Finally, the specific assumptions, values, and practices underlying the paradigm shift in special needs education are presented to flesh out our description of the emerging agenda for leaders in education.

Paradigms and Mental Models

Barker (1986), Osborne and Gaebler (1992), Perelman (1987), Peters (1985, 1987), Peters and Waterman (1982), and Wheatley (1992) have described paradigm shifts, first predicated by Thomas Kuhn (1970). These authors suggest that the power of paradigms lies in their ability to influence what we perceive. Paradigms are power-ful conceptual lenses that filter our individual and collective views of reality. Although Kuhn used *paradigm shift* to refer to dramatic shifts in conceptions of science, the term has more generally been used to describe changes in the ways people view their social worlds, including institutional practices in economic, political, and social systems, and their places in them. Barker (1986) has used the term to conclude that scientific and social communities can and do change paradigms when they adopt new models for viewing the world in light of new evidence that confounds their thinking.

According to Peters (1987), paradigm shifts in the business world include changes in perceptions of how people are viewed and val-ued in organizations, how those organizations are structured, how they are changing from centralized to decentralized semiautono-mous workplaces, and how leadership inspires self-management and continuous improvement fostered by a shared vision for the future. Kearns and Doyle (1988), Osborne and Gaebler (1992), Perelman (1987), and Davis and Botkin (1994) have extended think-ing about paradigm shifts to the public schools. They argue that the information-based society of the near future will force administra-tors to entirely restructure schools—not merely extend the school year or require more credits for graduation. The essential problem, they suggest, is that the hierarchically organized bureaucracy of public schools has destroyed the trust between administrators, teachers, and the lay public. This trust has been replaced by rules and regulations derived from federal and state mandates. Sage and Burrello (1994) describe an educational paradigm shift first pro-posed by Burrello and Lashley (1992), who drew from the works of several other researchers (Barker, 1986; Goodlad, 1984; Gregory & Smith, 1987; Kanter, 1983; Kearns & Doyle, 1988; Peters, 1987; Perelman, 1987; Senge, 1990). Their work describes a variety of struc-tural, policy, relational, and resource changes that are necessary if schools are to respond to the new demands made by a highly diverse, technological society.

Whereas a paradigm shift occurs across professional and research disciplines, individuals also experience dramatic changes in their perceptions of the world and their interactions with phenomena as well. Senge (1990) uses the term *mental models* to describe "deeply ingrained assumptions, generalizations, or even pictures or images that influence how we understand the world and how we take action" (p. 8). Mental models put opportunities and problems into perspective. They determine what information people perceive as relevant and useful in understanding and resolving the discrepancy between their actual situations and their goals. When individuals change their mental model, new alternatives for thought and action become evident that were previously screened out by well-established ways of thinking.

A new mental model of schooling has emerged from discussion of the purposes of education and the discourses we have encountered in our research on unified systems. The factors depicted in this evolutionary shift need to be considered in relation to one another, not merely as isolated instances. They should be viewed as interacting elements that support movement toward building a collegial culture for staff and students who are constantly redefining the structure of schools (Little, 1981; Little & McLaughlin, 1993).

Paradigm shifts and changing mental models are dynamic processes. In normal science and popular psychology, one paradigm or one mental model is exchanged for a new and improved version. We contend that this view is too simplistic for social sciences and education, which are multiparadigmatic and increasingly complex (House, 1981; Skrtic, 1991), and, in fact, natural scientists now recognize that such a view does not match the realities of the physical world either. For example, Wheatley (1992) characterizes the shift from Newtonian mechanics to quantum mechanics. She writes,

> Newtonian laws could not explain discoveries of strange worlds at the subatomic level, and the path was opened for new ways of comprehending the universe. While Newtonian mechanics still apply to our world and still contribute greatly to scientific advances, a new and different science is required to explain many phenomena. . . . Quantum mechanisms . . . does not describe a clock-like universe. (p. 33)

In the quantum world, relationships are all there is to reality. For the social scientist and educator, Wheatley adds,

> What is more important—the system or the individual? The quantum response is: "It depends." It is not an either/or question. There is no need to decide between the two. What is critical is the relationship created between the person and the set-

ting. That relationship will always be different, will always evoke different potentialities. It depends on the players and the moment. (p. 34)

If individuals and organizations are to continue to learn and grow, they must engage in ongoing examination, analysis, and transformation of mental models and paradigms. We advocate for an approach of inquiry-based critical pragmatism (Cherryholmes, 1988; Skrtic, 1991) in which practitioners continually examine their actions and the assumptions that support them to ensure that practices work and that they progress toward valued community ends. This approach provides a way of questioning basic assumptions, espoused theories, theories in use, and practices. Critical pragmatism, when it is applied to the professions, "is both a way of continually evaluating and re-appraising what a profession does (critical practice) and a way of continually re-appraising how it carries out such critical demands of its practice (critical discourse)" (Wheatley, p. 29). The goal is *self-formation;* "a pedagogical process of re-making ourselves" (p. 29) as educators discuss, relate to, and evaluate what they are doing and what they are becoming as an educational entity.

Justification of the Need for a Shift in Thinking About American Education

Since the 1983 publication of *A Nation at Risk*, many school districts and state departments of education have been engaging in strategic planning activities to demonstrate to stakeholders that they are dealing productively with the internal and external forces affecting their future. Many districts have engaged in school restructuring initiatives to illustrate that they are moving against the barriers to significant change in schools. School restructuring has many meanings, and to complicate matters further, it means different things to different stakeholder groups. School leaders must interpret those meanings as they relate to selected stakeholder groups, while setting a common direction and focus of the school district. Table 5.1 illustrates various interpretations of restructuring that have emerged from the literature.

For politicians, restructuring initially meant saving money by lowering taxes, and more recently, vouchers for private charter

TABLE 5.1
The Meaning of Restructuring Schools

	Recent Meaning	*Current Meaning*
Politicians/Business	Saving money and taxes through down-sizing	Charter schools, increased competition
Teachers/Unions	Empowerment	Loss of jobs to noncertified teachers in charter schools
Principals	Site-based management	Block scheduling and student choice
Superintendents/ Boards of education	Efficiencies and increased effectiveness	Losing students and dollars to private schools while maintaining the public option for all others
Public/Students	Higher graduation requirements, testing, and block scheduling	Choice and vouchers
Researchers	Changing the relationship of teaching and learning	Self-agency

schools. For teachers and teachers' unions, restructuring has meant teacher empowerment; more recently, these groups have battled advocates of privatization and public charter schools by arguing that these initiatives will result in fewer public resources for needy students and the hiring of noncertified teachers. For school principals, restructuring has meant site-based management and block scheduling, and more recently, losing students to other schools when choice options become available. For superintendents and board of education members, restructuring has meant increased efficiency and effectiveness, and more recently, losing students and resources if market based approaches win the day. For students and the public, restructuring has meant increased accountability through higher graduation requirements and more testing. To researchers, most notably Newmann and Wehlage (1996) and Louis and Kruse (1995), restructuring means changing the nature of teaching and learning. To us, transforming schools entails changing how educators and the public think about teaching and learning, students, educative relationships, and their participation in learning.

Many critics do not hold out much hope for public education. Davis and Botkin (1994) believe that only the romantics see the public schools as anachronisms that can be cast way. They suggest that radical change will require that alternatives be constructed (Nathan, 1996). Charter schools are an example of public schools that will "stop being all things educational to all citizens, like steel and other basic industries. Those who succeed in transforming themselves do so only by becoming smaller, more focused, and very agile in the limited markets they choose to serve" (Davis & Botkin, p. 133). Perelman (1992) argues that day has already come. He goes further to suggest that business has developed the knowledge base through hyperlearning technologies to deliver just in time learning opportunities to anyone, anywhere without that learning being mediated by a classroom teacher. Branson (1987) has argued that no single factor can ensure high quality and greater productivity in schools. The quick fixes of the past have yielded only limited and temporary results, he argues, because the traditional models of management, organized resource allocation, and innovation have become outmoded. Conventional fixes are single-variable remedies that often fail to lead to changes in the basic strategies of teaching and learning. And they do not focus on individualized, valued student outcomes. The problem, he continues, is not poor execution or insufficient resources; it is a flawed system design. "Little further improvement can be made in the traditional model of education without fundamental redesign; the productivity function in the American schools is near the upper attainable limit of achievement" (p. 16).

The public schools in many communities are failing more than 40% of their students. Schools focused on ordering and controlling a diverse student body through 12 grades of a sequential curriculum geared toward almost exclusively postsecondary education are failing the students, their families, and their communities. Advocates for restructuring are meeting resistance as they introduce their plans into the culture and program regularities of the district-centered decision making. Local school councils that include community participation threaten the prerogatives of the district power structure. Teachers are resisting multiage grouping and attempts to eliminate tracking by ability because they threaten traditional practices; parents resist because they feel that students with special needs will slow their children down. Instructional innovations like team teaching and cooperative learning are being resisted because they threaten teacher authority and the self-image of the educator (Sarason, 1982). Professionals bound within the bureaucracy subscribe to a paradigm of schooling that is based on a mechanistic, mass production model.

The search for ways to change the organizational design of public school has tempted educators and noneducators alike to look to management transformations in Japanese and European private enterprises. Deming's system of total quality management, the prescription that was touted in the 1990s, is valuable but limited (National LEADership Network Study Group on Restructured Schools, 1993). Perelman (1987) suggests that studying the ways in which private-sector organizations are instituting changes in management strategies is more valuable than studying the specific changes being made. Peters (1987) agrees that today there are no longer any excellent companies, that there are only good exemplars of organizations that are value and quality driven, that accept change and uncertainty as constants, and that are engaged in ongoing, continuous improvement. The challenge for educators is to determine which factors and systems within the control of individual school districts create obstacles to productive change and which factors support innovative, cooperative, choice-oriented work contexts for students, teachers, and school leaders.

The call for change, Johnson (1990) argues, will command the attention of teachers to the extent that it supports or compromises their current instructional practices. In her study of high school teachers in 16 districts, Johnson found that educators believed that the power to change their workplaces rested not in the hands of state-level policymakers but in their local schools and districts—among peers, principals, parents, and district administrators. For a change process to begin, there must be creative tension between current reality and future alternatives. The task for leaders is to create conditions for the school and community debate that may lead to a consensus that either reaffirms current reality or suggests a need for change.

Emerging Shifts in Thinking

According to Heifetz and Laurie (1997), the leadership task for educators is to get on the balcony and proclaim the future and the role of education in it. Burrello and Zadnik (1986) and Burrello, Lashley, and Van Dyke (1996) have argued that leadership counts— most significantly at the local level. A prime leadership role is to remind policymakers that school success is related to appreciating and accommodating differences at the margins as a means to increase the capacities of our teachers and school leadership to serve all students more appropriately and for participation in the economic, social, and political well-being of the community.

Changing paradigms of teaching and learning requires a knowledge of which changes are inherently compatible with the local culture, which ones are not, and which ones can, over time and with support, be reinvented to fit evolving norms of practice. Senge (1990) suggests that, in addition to engaging in systems-level thinking, educators must confront their own shared vision of schooling. Until teachers are given the opportunity to engage in open dialogues about the future while realistically examining the current state of schooling, they will thwart any change. It would be foolish to believe that teachers and individual school communities will adopt any new model of schooling without this dialogue. It is only when we come to understand the strongly held values of members of school faculties and of communities at large can we begin to understand how to change them.

Once the difference between the real state of affairs and the transformed school is defined, a school community can begin to build toward a shared vision of what it hopes to create. In Senge's terms, a learning organization can begin to emerge. A learning organization should be founded on a consensus in which all staff members find meaning in the common vision of the organization and their places in it (Senge, 1990). Shared visions grow out of new mental models of practice, which, in turn, are based on a commitment to team learning. If schools are to truly become learning organizations, they must cast off mistrust and governance by rule making and move toward becoming organizations bounded by a shared vision and shared values. Teachers and school leaders must design their own mental models or paradigms of practice, using team learning and systems-level thinking and action. They must come to understand that the systems they create, like the ones that they inherited, demand constant evaluation and revision to eliminate behaviors that may have unintended side effects.

Creating the Local Dialogue

Determining the purpose of education is a conversation in which boards of education, superintendents, and indeed all educators need to continually engage their communities. We have offered Postman's (1995) narratives as examples of discourses that transcend the individual and provide purpose and meaning to the pursuit of an education. As we consider his narratives within the context of current educational discourse, we find the traditional purposes of school serving the false gods of economic utility and technology. These purposes reduce or hinder other important individual development, social and communal purposes that are significant for students. Traditional school purposes also neglect the need for education to make sense in light of the interests and concerns students bring to the school setting. Finally, the traditional purposes of education neglect the educative role that schools must play in communities in a vibrant, democratic society.

Superintendents and boards of education must have this discussion to raise awareness of the mental models of schooling within their communities. Our models, or espoused theories, and our practices, or theories in action, guide the conclusions we draw, the assumptions we hold, the interpretations we make, and the data we select from our conversations, interactions, observations, study, and reflections. Helping one another find meaning and facilitate action is at the heart of surfacing and challenging the beliefs and values we all bring to the teaching and learning enterprise. Engaging productively in this kind of public discourse requires that communities confront various purposes of education and that they put forth some guidance about what they want from the education of their children.

Traditional Schools

The basis of learning that underlies traditional teacher-centered schools is positivist and behaviorally oriented. Traditional schools are primarily concerned with normative behavior and group processing of students through a prescribed curriculum. Given their fundamental purposes to select and sort students into postschool careers and educational opportunities, the most appropriate metaphor is the machine or mass production line (Morgan, 1997). The image of learning as mass production, divided up by subject or grade level, age cohort, or ability groups, conjures up students moving through a production line on a conveyor belt. Each student is expected to meet prescribed expectations in a particular way for each teacher.

Teachers shape and mold student character through disciplined study of substantive knowledge, which may or may not have an immediate consequence, long-term use, or meaning for the student. The student assumes that the teacher is an expert who possesses knowledge that is necessary for success, and the student is reinforced for attaining some level of approximation of that knowledge through academic skill and personal motivation. In this model, knowledge is transmitted from teacher to student, and the knowledge of the teacher and the means of transmission are subject to manipulation. However, effectiveness in knowledge transmission is primarily a function of the student's ability to receive and absorb that which has been transmitted. Curriculum and instruction flows from a deterministic position in which the curriculum is preordained through competencies or prescribed outcomes by grade levels. Teachers codify the curriculum in textbooks for easy reference. More recently, teachers have had to attend to state-prescribed proficiencies. Instruction is most often teacher-directed instruction, through question-and-answer formats, in which student seatwork is the primary means of practice and knowledge building for the student.

The traditional assessment process follows the deterministic, preordained curriculum model and uses both teacher-made and standardized tests to select and sort students. Testing can be used as formative evaluation to influence instruction and assist the teacher in determining review and enrichment activities for individual students. However, alignment between learning outcomes, assessment, and instruction is usually very loose, and knowledge and generalization are not considered priorities. Students are taught and learn isolated from one another, other teachers, and other subjects and classes.

Traditional schools are organized as professional bureaucracies that control the distribution of influence and decision making through a hierarchy of relationship and positions. People occupying those positions feel that the office entitles them to levels of responsibility and authority within prescribed boundaries given to them by even higher authority in the organization. As a result, the change process is essentially top-down and occurs as a response to an external authority or significant political interest group. Change develops from what is known and from the center outward—slowly and deliberately. Typically, a pilot project is envisioned, and the change is led by power brokers and leveraged by limited local dollars. Once a pilot project is under way, most school districts are often unable to guarantee that succeeding schools will have the same time and coterie of resources—human and material—to provide support for the change.

Restructuring Schools

The school restructuring movement is primarily concerned with higher-order thinking and substantive knowledge acquisition and use. It is driven by instrumental purposes related to postschool outcomes in an information society. Although social processes of learning are acknowledged, the school restructuring movement does not see them necessarily as an end in themselves. Rather, social processes are seen as means to facilitate individual achievement and economic productivity.

Restructuring advocates suggest that both cognitive and cooperative learning theories promote learning because students must interact with knowledge in order to add it to their personal repertoires. Although learning basic skills is a prerequisite, the goal of learning is critical thinking and applying that thinking to problem-solving activities. In these models, students are active participants in the learning process, and teachers are facilitators who create opportunities for learning. The brain or information processing metaphor drives the restructuring advocates. If schools would raise their expectations and focus on cognitive processing of information and problem solving, they would be more successful in preparing schools for postschool life and postsecondary education institutions. The brain metaphor or information-processing metaphor suggests an input-processing-output model of learning where students receive information that they process to a level of understanding that affects the product produced. In addition, restructuring advocates argue that traditional approaches have not expected enough of students (therefore the need for higher standards) and that traditional assessment approaches do not adequately measure whether students have learned important and useful knowledge (thus calling for performance-based assessment).

Schools engaged in restructuring are primarily concerned about mastery and challenging intellectual materials. The curriculum tends to be prescribed with some room for student interests. It is largely discipline bound, organized into discrete courses, and clearly geared to postsecondary prerequisites. Discussions of curricular integration typically involve instruction in areas where disciplinary boundaries overlap. Learning outcomes and expectations are more closely aligned.

Authentic instruction focuses on higher-level thinking skills and substantive conversations with teachers, colleagues, and peers inside and beyond the school (see Newmann & Wehlage, 1996). Authentic pedagogy is used as a means to create meaningful standards across disciplines. Authentic achievement includes the construction of knowledge, disciplined inquiry, and value beyond the school. Assessment tasks emphasize organization of information and consideration of alternatives to gauge the student's ability to construct knowledge. To measure the student's abilities in disciplined inquiry, assessments emphasize content, process, and elaborate written communication. Gauging value involves assessing the student's ability to transfer knowledge to problems beyond the school and performances before groups of stakeholders.

In schools that are restructuring, power is devolved to the school level for certain allocated sets of decisions. Groups of teachers selected by either the principal or their peers select the direction of the school. These site-based teams engage in problem-solving student and teacher issues, determining priorities, allocating budgets, and developing school improvement or personnel development plans. Restructuring schools advocates have argued for individual school site development and adaptation of innovations. The goal has been school site development rather than system development. Many restructuring efforts involve transferring models of practice from the literature to practice.

Transforming Schools

In our view of transforming schools, the primary purpose of education is the preparation of students for all aspects of postschool life, including lifelong learning and growth. We are preoccupied with students making intelligent choices that reflect their interests in the context of the larger community. The goal is self-management and self-advocacy, which demand active student engagement and construction of meaningful work, based on performance of consensually agreed-upon public criteria.

Both the traditional and restructured models are deterministic and require the teacher to do something to or for the student. In our view, these approaches leave an important actor in the educational narrative out of the discourse about learning—the student. Transforming schools use multiple theoretical perspectives to inform a more personalized approach to student learning. Since the goal is self-management in a more diverse global society, these schools value the active construction of meaning and transfer of learning to demonstrable tasks. Students use their peers to test their thinking and get feedback from their teachers in an iterative inquiry process of problem definition, problem analysis, hypothesis generation, research for arguments and findings, discussion, concept maps, and presentation of written and oral reports.

A transforming school goes beyond cognitive theory to assess how individual students process information and use social contexts to enhance learning. The metaphor of the school as a living organism is more appropriate to transforming schools. An organism adapts and evolves through its experience and relationship to its environment. Intelligence is defined here as the ability to adapt to one's environment and thrive. The organism metaphor suggests continuous growth and self-organizing. If lifelong learning is to be enhanced, the individual must become the self-organizing unit seeking his/her own direction and exploration.

In transforming schools, the key directional change is moving from a solely preordinate and prescribed curriculum to student-based project learning that blurs disciplinary boundaries. The curriculum is negotiated through a school and community conversation about essential outcomes and essential personal learning goals. The student is involved in convincing both teachers and parents that her learning is critical to her future and is sustainable. Students have more responsibility to describe and defend their selections and to demonstrate satisfactory performance on mutually determined quality indicators. In a transforming school, Newmann's concepts of authentic pedagogy, achievement, and assessment are paramount. The difference is that the assessment includes the learner in developing the quality indicators and rubrics to be used. The learner is required to apply these indicators to both teacher-directed tasks and activities as well as to her own project-learning tasks. Assessments are both self-referenced and criterion-referenced. Normative assessment is a separate and distinct activity in these schools and is not the primary driving force in the curriculum or instruction. Assessments are conducted to meet three purposes: (a) to measure students' learning, (b) to help teachers and students decide what is working and what is not, and (c) to build action plans that ensure that student learning continues.

In the transforming school, teams of semiautonomous teachers organize themselves into distinct groups that take responsibility for the whole range of academic and social outcomes for students. School leaders spend most of their time creating a Senge dialogue that creates a tension around what is or was versus what must become for students, families, and schools. Transforming schools requires examining the mental models present in the school and building teams of teachers committed to examine how they learn and how to make student learning continuous and meaningful. Creating semiautonomous teams of learners, students, and teachers having control over what and how students learn and an authentic and public accountability process are the key to creating empowered students and teachers and, parenthetically, a learning organization.

A transformational mental model requires an understanding of the relationship between teaching and learning. Educators and community members who are interested in transforming schools in these ways must address these questions as they conduct a school and community dialogue:

1. What do students need to know and be able to do? What dispositions or attitudes are critical to understand their place in an increasingly diverse and interconnected world?
2. How will students come to know what they need to know or learn how to do what they need to do? How will students inquire about what they need to know and be able to do?
3. How will teachers, community members, parents, and peers help students learn?
4. What resources will students need to engage in meaningful learning?
5. How will students demonstrate that they have knowledge or can use it to perform tasks, solve problems, and inquire further?

School leaders who engage their communities in a dialogue about the future must consider the following questions:

1. Who must be included in the discussion? What is expected from those who participate?
2. How will the unique differences of the participants be reflected in the discourse and in the decisions that result?
3. What are the tensions between the mental models of schooling that exist in the community?
4. What instructional approaches are appropriate to use? How will these approaches draw optimum performances from students?
5. How will student performance be assessed? How will the logistics of personalized assessment be managed?
6. Which audiences will be involved in student assessment, and how will their roles and perspectives be included in summative evaluations of the student's educational performance?

School leaders whose style is hierarchical will not be successful in leading their communities through the dialogue necessary for transforming schools. School leaders must also change their mental models of leadership to reflect the democratic, pragmatic, and critical stances inherent in transforming schooling as we have described. A new metaphor for leadership must replace the school commandant and charismatic visionary approaches that dominated our conceptions of schooling in the 20th century. We recommend the metaphor of the playhouse as our conception of the work of school leaders as they strive to transform their schools.

The School as Playhouse

Our thoughts about transforming schools leads us to assert that new schools need to use the theater or playhouse as a working metaphor. The playhouse produces a variety of works in any one season. The superintendent of schools, like the executive director of the playhouse, needs to screen and select a script. Playwrights create texts that can yield a variety of interpretations, and in fact some plays are written to invite an array of perspectives on the story and characters and to engage the audience in a thoughtful reading and reflection on the meaning of the text for their own lives.

The superintendent as executive producer needs to assess his board of directors and community to determine which playwright's script fits their community's history, culture, and aspirations for itself and its members. The executive must also assess the availability of human talent and other resources necessary to produce each of the particular plays selected.

Imagine now a superintendent with three playwrights, each espousing one of the three views of schooling and their corresponding narratives. The traditional playwright uses his nostalgia about the past to focus on the basics, student discipline, and attitudes of respect for authority. The restructuring playwright uses information processing and a higher-order thinking skills message to argue for preparation for postschool life and higher education for all. This playwright sees school as a social instrument for economic independence and technical competence. The transformational playwright offers a third interpretation of the purpose of education and how it plays out on the school stage. He is promoting a story of empowerment, self-advocacy, and community building. He sees the promise of life, liberty, and the pursuit of happiness.

Which play and narrative will the superintendent and staff promote? Using the set of questions posed earlier, which criteria will the superintendent offer for board members to consider in selecting a narrative? Are they mutually exclusive? Which plays first, second, third—or not at all? Once the play is selected, the executive producer has to translate the play into real terms for the associate producers and ultimately the director.

Directors interpret their understandings about a play to stage managers, technicians, and actors. The frontline talent then extends those interpretations, delving into motivations, themes, and story lines, until the play is ready for presentation to the audience. As a result of these varying levels of interpretation and collaborative rendering of the playwright's text, the cast and crew come to understand the playwright's story and how their characters and roles influence the points the playwright is trying to make. By opening night, the production has grown from the playwright's black-and-white text to the company's live performance.

To be successful, the playhouse must provide an inclusionary setting that is mindful of all the actors and their needs to belong and learn what it means to be a member of the company. The company must have a transcending purpose upon which trust can be built so that each member feels free to contribute in whatever ways he or she believes necessary to the performance. So, too, must schools have an overarching purpose that fosters trust, contribution, and learning in all members of the educational company. Regardless of which play and which script is chosen, we suggest that Postman's (1995) narratives be used to provide transcending purposes related to the education of students with disabilities for teachers, students, and community members. Two of the narratives that include rather than exclude are (a) the unfinished agenda of the American experiment and (b) diversity and people with disabilities.

The unfinished agenda narrative speaks to the evolution of the American experiment in self-rule. This narrative asks, "Who is to participate in the American dream of life, liberty, and pursuit of happiness?" In a country that absorbs most of the world's immigrants annually, how can we continue to deny our own citizens the fruits of the democracy? The American experiment is ongoing. Students with disabilities have been guaranteed certain of those unalienable rights as citizens, yet those rights are abridged daily in school districts across the country. Facilitating a discussion about the unfinished agenda enables school leaders to put the struggle to educate students with disabilities into the context of American schooling.

The second question of this narrative is, How do we define participation in our community? How do we learn to participate? Postman (1995) writes that schools prepare students for two seemingly contradictory purposes—first, learning about the world's cultures, rules, requirements, constraints, and prejudices and inculcating them into the students' patterns of thought and behavior; second, criticizing these very same conditions and becoming independent thinkers who are "distanced from conventional wisdom of their time and with the strength to question, and [the] skill to change what needs to be changed" (p. 60). If we were to track the history of inclusion of persons with disabilities, we could clearly identify a series of thinkers and activists who challenged the conventional wisdom of community leaders over the past 225 years of the republic regarding who should and should not participate in the American experiment. Defining participation requires that students understand how they come to think about who is valued in American society and how social justice has been transgressed by exclusionary practices.

Postman (1995) also offers the diversity narrative to provide a transcending purpose for inclusion and dialogue about persons with disabilities. The language of "able-ness" rather than disability, the placement of emphasis on personhood rather than the impairment, and use of the term *handicapped* to illustrate how obstacles affect performance are all examples that will help students and teachers understand diversity. In many communities, the disabled may be the only examples of diversity a school staff might have to bring a more increasingly differentiated world home to students. We recall the principal of a school near Austin, Texas, who fought to get a class of students with significant cognitive and physical disabilities included in her school because she believed her student body needed the diversity of experience these students could bring to the school. All her students needed an inclusive language and cultural experience to help them understand the meaning of able-ness, disability, and handicap, and their applications to learning and community experience. Postman believes these discussions

> must be done delicately. . . . We must proceed with the knowledge that many students and their parents believe their story is the literal truth. There is no need to dispute them. The idea is to show that different people have told different stories; that they

have, at various times, borrowed elements from one another's narratives; that it is appropriate to treat the narratives of others with respect; and that, ultimately, all such narratives have a similar purpose. (p. 154)

The diversity narrative compels us to understand how simultaneously variable and similar all humans are.

In transforming schools, principals, teachers, and instructional staff consider a variety of instructional practices and policies (i.e., educational texts) with which students interact. Principals broadly interpret the meanings of these texts and integrate them with the core values and purposes important to the school. Teachers and support personnel work with the texts to make them practical—understandable for students and constituent audiences concerned about what students are doing. Students then engage these texts and make them their own. They integrate their extant knowledge and experience with new knowledge and experiences to produce interpretations that can be viewed by those who are interested in their progress as learners. Over time, the practices and policies generated for and by the school become live performances and other observable evidence that have meaning for students' lives. To be successful, the school needs a transcending narrative—a vision of purposes and outcomes and a framework for discussions—just as a playhouse needs a script.

Transforming schools requires resources, thought, and motivation to learn in the same way that producing a play requires money, interpretation, and the artist's interest in creating a story about life. School personnel, students, and communities that engage in transformation understand their roles and relationships differently. They see themselves involved in a collaborative enterprise that produces results important to their lives and continued learning. The plays they present are works in progress that reflect and change meaning for those who live in the communities in which they occur.

6

The New Work of
Leadership in Unified Schools

In this chapter, we continue to build on our experiences consulting with practitioners and evaluating programs throughout the nation to describe how the elements of a learner-centered discourse give rise to a unified service system that responds to the needs of all students. We believe in a systems-oriented perspective that is based on (a) a core ideology (core values and purpose); (b) the commitment of leadership, staff, and community members to a learner-centered vision; (c) the use of core technologies implemented within a total quality perspective; and (d) recognition of the complexity of a school's culture and the process of change. The systems thinking of Senge (1990) and his associates helps us understand how two systems archetypes explain the relationship between general and special education and the management options available to leadership to get the systems back in balance and harmony. Wheatley (1997) has taught us that authors merely create the white space that many practitioners already have identified as new ways of organizing human endeavor. We think the new work of leadership is to trust in the instincts of those practitioners who in many schools have begun to implement selected learner-centered practices. This chapter is dedicated to our practicing colleagues who have taught us how they think about schools in new ways and how they are moving their practices toward the vision outlined in the learner-centered discourse.

Systems Thinking

System Archetypes

Senge's (1990) system archetypes are the means leaders use to bring systems thinking to bear on the patterns of a practice. System archetypes are the practice patterns that help leaders manage both *detail complexity*—examining multiple variables simultaneously— and *dynamic complexity*—"determining the cause and effect between variables and events that are not close in time and *when* obvious interventions do not produce expected outcomes" (p. 364). These practices are tools to help leaders and followers alike determine the interconnectedness of a system.

We have selected two archetypes from Senge (1990) that we believe inform thinking systemically about the failure of the public school system to deal with diversity and disability in its student population. These archetypes illustrate the need for long-term solutions rather than short-term fixes. They require the participants themselves to build their own solutions and self-regulating mechanisms to prevent regression to program regularities (Sarason, 1982). Examples of those regularities are a mechanistic batch-processing structure that sorts and selects students based on ability levels, fixed schedules, the power relationships that determine teacher and student roles, a bounded subject-matter-oriented curriculum, and, more recently, the addition of normative, high-stakes testing.

System Archetype 1: Shifting the Burden

Skrtic (1991) has argued that special services have been receiving the failures of the public school system because these students cannot compete within a typical program that is geared to meet the academic needs of achieving and well-adjusted students. The pressure to continue finding alternative placements for students outside the mainstream increases as the stakes for graduation are raised through state standardized examinations. The rapid rise of alternative school placements (for "bad actors"—students who need an alternative) and special services is leading to three types of public education arrangements. First, the majority program (60%) is for those achieving students and those who accommodate themselves to the system; second, the alternative programs (10%) have been developed for students who act out or have alternative learning styles; and third, special service programs (15%) are required for students with mild-to-significant disabilities. In addition to these students, we would argue that another 15% are underperforming in the majority system.

The burden to serve students who are not succeeding—students at risk, students with identified disabilities, disruptive students—is shifted to the special services subsystems. Special services were originally organized to provide a continuum of services from in-class support to out-of-school and homebound placements to provide the total educational program for these students (Deno, 1970). The short-term problem brought about by these students was remediation. If remediation was successful, the students were returned to the classroom without further support. From a systems-thinking perspective, Senge (1990) argues that "as this correction is used more and more, more fundamental long-term corrective measures are used less and less. Over time, the capabilities for the fundamental solution may atrophy or become disabled, leading to greater reliance on the symptomatic solution" (p. 381). Shifting the burden to the intervenor, according to Senge, results in the host system's never learning how to deal with the problems themselves, as has been the case in the parallel system of special education, which has assumed total responsibility for educating the "exceptional student."

The early warning signs that shifting the burden has occurred are expansion of the student groups considered to be at risk and made eligible for special accommodations outside the classroom programs for typical students. The narrower the definition of who is considered normal and capable in terms of academic, social, and emotional success, the higher the referral and placement rate in the alternative systems. The almost total transfer of responsibility for working with these students is now outside the regular system.

In addition, the parallel system of special services itself becomes a separate bureaucracy and starts to move in a direction of its own. The original intent to return students to the mainstream or to help them compete for employment and a life outside of school may be severely impaired by their experiencing separate standards of performance, separate curricula, and separate accountability measures. We know these unanticipated outcomes have already occurred, making the need for system unification a priority for creating equity and excellence for all students. If we do not educate students with special needs appropriately now, we will create new problems down the line.

Management Principles

Senge offers two management principles for the school-community leadership to consider. First, he argues that leaders should concentrate on the fundamental solution: How can teachers and school leaders plan and better educate all students inclusively rather than shifting the burden to special services? Given the time and resources, how might they find a fundamental solution to educate all students more effectively? His second management principle is "teach people to fish, rather than giving them fish." He suggests focusing on enhancing capabilities of the regular system to solve its own problems. If outside help is needed, it should restrict itself to learning how to help people in the regular system develop their own skills, resources, and infrastructure to be more capable in the future.

In cases of shifting the burden, a form of system addiction and dependency on the parallel system requires increasing resources to support the host system and its subsystems. Other implications of shifting the burden include eroding standards and goals, narrowing the definition and scope of acceptable behavior, abusing the referral and evaluation process, and overuse of the system by selected teachers, principals, parents, and other community agencies. All these other examples lead to escalation of needs and the growth of the competing parallel system, which further stretches limited resources.

System Archetype 2: The Tragedy of the Commons

In this system archetype, Senge (1990) argues that individuals or groups "use a commonly available but limited resource solely on the basis of individual or group need. At first they are rewarded for using it; eventually, they get diminishing returns, which causes them to intensify their efforts. Eventually, the resource is either significantly depleted, eroded, or entirely used up" (p. 387). The early warning signs of the Tragedy of the Commons as it plays out in public schools are (a) there are no longer spots available for everyone in the special services system or the alternative schools; (b) parents and teachers are pleased that the identified children are getting the help they need to succeed; (c) the remaining students can proceed without impediment; (d) jobs are being created for specialists; and (e) unions are seen as protecting teachers' working conditions.

When things begin to get out of proportion and costs rise dramatically, districts cannot keep paying the bills. Districts are required to provide the services that IEP committees design without being held accountable for the services the committees recommended. Often, service recommendations include using paraprofessionals for in-class or in-school support to such an extent that parents are now expecting one-on-one instruction. This is expensive and can be in opposition to other outcomes such as developing student independence and success in school and later in postschool life. The current solution is for special service personnel to take more students.

Management Principles

Senge suggests that managing and preventing the Tragedy of the Commons require educating everyone and creating forms of self-regulation and peer pressure to change practices. In addition, state and local leadership may reduce use of the limited resources being held in common through regulations and compliance monitoring. Ideally, any local solution should be designed by the local participants themselves.

As more and more students require special services, the general education system is reaching the limits of its capacity. System redesign at the school-site level may involve teacher teams designing unique approaches to meet student needs and to increase their capacity to serve students with diverse needs. Teacher teams negotiate for additional district resources, including direct support and training. These teams are also required to manage the resources they generate. Resources are finite, and teachers are accountable for the decisions their colleagues make in joint deliberations and by their shared responsibility to serve all students appropriately. The aim is to assign and be responsible for all students in the school they would attend with their age-appropriate brothers and sisters. Special services personnel help co-teach any students who need unique accommodations until teachers and peers can help them succeed without support.

Using concepts like minimum specifications, student and teacher teams are challenged to create new forms of organization that are more individually student oriented and allow the diversity of the student population to follow more than one path to success in meeting expectations. Teachers and students are held accountable for demonstrating progress toward valued student outcomes. Essentially, schools must be designed for differentiation rather than standardization (Darling-Hammond, 1993).

The Elements of Transformation

Core Ideology

Collins and Porras (1996) have defined *core ideology* as the core values and purposes of an organization. They are the essential building blocks of any high-performing system that requires the effective use of intellectual capital. They also signal what an individual school's adaptive response might be as the staff manages the tension between competing policy perspectives, such as the continuum of services and learner-centered schools. They serve as the means to reach a shared vision of the ends of education that must acknowledge diverse learners while coping with a rapid increase in the knowledge base, an increase in higher expectations, the use of knowledge management technology, and the need for continual improvement in the teaching workforce.

Garmston and Wellman (1995) believe schools foster learning to adapt to core values and the district vision by continuing to base decisions on the responses to two recurring questions: (a) Who are we? (b) What is our purpose? Filtering district- and school-level responses through a set of core assumptions that drive the self-organization necessary to build enrollment in the core values and vision include

- Shifting decision-making responsibility and authority to the people most influenced by the decision
- Setting outcomes and standards that signal a passion for excellence and attention to the qualities that are based on real-world needs
- Supporting faculty members in collaboratively setting and working toward self-defined goals (p. 8)

Transformation to a learner-centered schools perspective begins with an articulation of underlying core values and purposes.

Core Values

Core values that support an accompanying ideology are what distinguish high-performing organizations from lower-performing organizations. We believe that four or five core values are sufficient to frame the shared vision necessary for a learner-centered school. These core values must, moreover, serve as the calling that binds faculty, students, and parents inextricably together in their hearts and souls. The core values that need discussion and consensus within the district to support the transformation to learner-centered schools and a unified delivery system might include the following:

1. As educators, we respect the dignity of students' unique sociocultural history and are committed to the fulfillment of their human possibilities.

John Gardner (1987) has written,

There is nothing more crucial to the renewal of a social system then the effectiveness and capacity, the quality and vitality of the human beings flowing into the system. These are chiefly the young people coming out of our schools and colleges to take their adult place in the adult world. They will be the creators of our future. . . . The release of human potential is and must be always a central value. (pp. 10-11)

2. Educators should nurture a sense of public duty in students to continually reconstruct the community of which they are part.

The students must become committed to a continual re-weaving of the social fabric.

Again, Gardner (1987) has said,

This task is not one of uncritical reaffirmation; it is a task of renewal. The process of renewal encompasses both continuity and change, reinterpreting tradition to meet new conditions, building a better future on an acknowledged heritage. (pp. 13-14)

3. Teachers are first and foremost mentors and coaches who are committed to the continual improvement of learning for all students and their colleagues in the school.

As learners take increasingly more responsibility for their own learning, teachers use standards to guide them toward valued common outcomes, incorporate individual student goals, and assess progress by continually disaggregating performance data for each individual in order to select appropriate learning opportunities.

4. A school district becomes a learning community when it invites its students, faculty, staff, and community members to create settings in which personal mastery flourishes, where common bonds form, where all are engaged in team learning, and where enhancing the welfare of all those who work and learn there is the driving ideological force.

Gardner (1987) closes with this concern: Releasing human potential

must reach beyond the schools and permeate the whole society. It must be reflected in our programs for children whose potentialities may be blighted through crippling illness or severe sensory handicaps or environmental deprivation. It must be reflected in the workplace, in leisure activities, even in retirement planning. What is wanted is an attitude, widely shared throughout the society, toward individual growth, development, and learning the context of our shared values—an attitude that is fiercely impatient with impediments to healthy growth and that never ceases to seek out the undiscovered possibilities in each of us. (p. 12)

A set of core values like those described above supports a set of core purposes and a learner-centered vision—a "good-enough vision"—that enables members of the school-community to begin work toward the outcomes they choose to pursue.

Core Purposes

Core purposes should be inclusive of all students, geared toward lifelong learning, and oriented toward creating a public that is responsible to maintain and extend the benefits of a democratic society. We expect that all students will demonstrate different levels of competency and that mastery is a lifelong pursuit that is not restricted by high school graduation. Our core purpose, then, is to empower learners to sustain a just, democratic society and thrive in a more diverse and competitive world by advocating for their beliefs, representing their ideas in meaningful ways, and demonstrating their skills in a variety of settings.

Learners are effective if they can

- Demonstrate character through honesty, personal courage, and compassion and respect for others
- Function independently
- Think critically and creatively
- Communicate their beliefs and ideas meaningfully to others
- Cooperate and teach others
- Use appropriate resources to seek, access, and use their knowledge in postschool settings
- Exhibit self-confidence by taking risks
- Create options for themselves and others
- Be responsible and accountable while making informed choices

Core Technologies

The core technologies of a learner-centered model of schooling are informed by *Learner-Centered Principles: A Framework for School Redesign and School Organization* (APA, 1995). The core technologies that drive the school-community dialogue between staff, parents, and students support a learner-centered discourse and the unification of human and fiscal resources to support each learner.

Community of Learners' Classroom Vision

Brown and Campione (1990, 1996, 1998) have written extensively about a community of learners where mutual responsibility abides and reciprocal learning occurs. They suggest that students in a community of learners' classroom are encouraged to engage in self-reflective learning and critical inquiry. Students act as researchers (collectively and individually) who are responsible, to a larger and larger extent (from preschool through high school) for defining their own knowledge and expertise. In this type of classroom, teachers act as

> responsive guides to students' discovery processes . . . [and] . . . provide instruction on a need-to-know basis which allows them to respond to students' needs, rather than to a fixed scope and sequence schedule or an inflexible lesson plan . . . the content of the curriculum features a few recurring themes that students come to understand at increasingly sophisticated levels of explanatory coherence and theoretical generality. (1998, p. 153)

If technology is used, it is primarily a means for students to do research, structure "what if" scenarios, display data, and prepare high-quality reports. Drill and practice applications are used for those students who need additional practice and repetition to gain fluency and mastery. But for the most part, technology is used to foster intentional learning through reflection and discussion with their peers. Finally, in the community of learners' classroom, methods of assessment are clear to learners because they participate in designing and selecting the appropriate quality indicators that meet the evaluation standards set in consultation with their teachers. The purpose of assessment is to focus on the students' ability to discover and use knowledge, demonstrate a skill, or transfer their learning to other problems or settings rather than focusing on basic retention or static measures of product.

Common Outcomes

Transformation to a learner-centered model can be resisted and threatened by many insiders and outsiders for the same reasons. We have seen faculties and community members struggle with the curricular and instructional changes inherent in a learner-centered model primarily because they are used to teacher autonomy and parental control. Empowering students to have more responsibility for their own learning is frightening to both teachers and parents. Brown and Campione (1998) suggest that developmental psychologists now believe that early behaviorists "severely underestimated young children's capacities . . . [of having] limited attention spans, deemed incapable of inferential reasoning, of certain forms of classification, and of insightful learning and transfer" (p. 155). They believed that children in schools should have been required to "work to mastery on decontextualized skills for short periods of time under conditions of positive and negative reinforcement" (p. 155). Many teachers and parents were raised in schools that were influenced by these notions, and they have a hard time making a shift to new ideas about learning.

Curriculum is bounded by state and local school district outcomes that identify the standards that all children should strive to know and live up to. In addition, students should have the dispositions that shape the attitudes and character that a democracy demands of its people as they pursue collective as well as individual happiness. We have found that the Vermont State Standards provide an excellent set of exemplar outcome standards that are both comprehensive and open to interpretation. They have been criticized by the American Federation of Teachers (Olson, 1999) for not being specific enough. Yet we think these standards provide sufficient "white space" to allow teachers to create multiple ways of thinking and trying to meet them with their students. Brown and Campione argue that to "select enduring themes for discussion and to revisit them often, each time at an increasingly more mature level of understanding" (p. 161) is what Bruner (1963) had in mind when he wrote about a spiraling curriculum. Brown and Campione (1998) use biology as an example to illustrate this point: "School children become increasingly interested in crosscutting themes that would form the basis of an understanding of such principles as metabolic rate, reproduction strategies, and structural and behavioral adaptations" (p. 161).

Individual Outcomes

The learner-centered classroom model is driven by state and local common outcomes but equally by individual student outcomes. Individual outcomes determined by students and parents in consultation with the teacher are the students' unique interpretation of how they will both satisfy the community's interests as well as their individual interests. Students' choice of outcomes and their individual approaches to meeting them is a key element in the core technology of learning.

Once students, their parents, and their teachers lay out their semester or yearlong plans, the real individual planning, implementation, and continual evaluation begins. Students need to create a weekly or bimonthly plan that they implement under the guidance of their teachers. While direct instruction continues on a regular basis in response to individual needs, students engage in regular projects that structure their learning of selected standards for the semester. Students are expected to assess their learning weekly, based on feedback from their teachers and peers. They are also expected to track their progress along with preordinate rubrics and record their findings in the classroom electronic support systems.

The educational management system is the backbone of the information system used by the student and teacher to track progress and to make modifications after they receive feedback from the home. Quarterly, the parent joins the student and teacher to compare intent with actual performance and the predetermined quality indicators expected. Teachers collect authentic assessment and feedback data each quarter and annually create action planning cycles and adjust outcomes and instruction for each student. The learner-centered individual planning process is the centerpiece of the learner-centered classroom model.

Lynn Murray, Al Myers, and their colleagues in Williston, Vermont, have worked toward a vision of learner-centered schools. They believe that the key to their success is to

respect kids and respect their abilities to make decisions for themselves. And you have to change your role from being the person with all the information and holding all the strings to the person who is willing to be on the sides coaching, guiding and supporting kids. (Burrello, 1999)

Most of all, Murray and Myers have taught us that real transformation to a learner-centered school can be done if educators engage students and their parents as partners who make the right choices for themselves, based on teacher input and feedback.

The teachers and principals in the *For Our Students, For Ourselves* (Burrello, 1996) project have taught us that their movement toward learner-centered principles did not begin until they finally confronted their own need to know why students learn the way they do. Carol Porter expressed it best for the Mundelein High School District (suburban Chicago) staff:

> We knew what was good for kids. We really had some gut feelings about what learning looks like. But I don't know at that point, that we knew the "why" behind the decisions that we're making. I was at a point in my career, where I was ready for that "why." I had experimented with "how" and but I didn't really know why, I was thirsty for that "why." (Burrello, 1996)

Summary of the Vision. Brown and Campione (1998) offer six concepts that overlap with the 12 learner-centered principles to highlight the unique aspects of this kind of vision. First, they emphasize that in this classroom depiction learning is active, strategic, self-conscious, self-motivated, and purposeful. They believe this overstatement is necessary because, since the early part of the 20th century, the belief "that rote memory trains the mind; advocates of fact acquisition stalk the land" (p. 178). Second, learner-centered classrooms create multiple zones of proximal development with students learning at different rates and with appetites to learn in some arenas and not in others. They argue for pushing students to the upper bounds of potential for each task.

Third, learner-centered classrooms should legitimize diversity and differences between students. They write,

> It is very much our intention to increase diversity because traditional classrooms have aimed at just the opposite, decreasing diversity, a traditional practice based upon several assumptions: that there exist prototypical, normal students who, at a certain age, can do a certain amount of work, or grasp a certain amount of material, in the same amount of time. There is little that we know about learning and development that support

these assumptions. Therefore, although we must aim at conformity on the basics, *almost* everyone must read eventually, we must also aim at increasing diversity of expertise and interests so that members of the community can benefit from the increasing richness of the knowledge available. The essence of teamwork is pooling varieties of expertise. Teams composed of members with homogeneous ideas and skills are denied access to such diversity. (p. 179)

The fourth element in learner-centered classrooms is its dialogical base. These classrooms provide explicit opportunity for student voices to be heard as well as to share a discourse and common knowledge and individual expertise. Again, according to Brown and Campione (1996),

Dialogues provide the format for novices to adopt the discourse structure, goals, values, and belief systems of scientific practice. Over time, the community of learners adopt a common voice and common knowledge base, a shared system of meaning, beliefs, and activity that is as often implicit as it is explicit. The significance of including diverse learners only makes the dialogue inclusive of issues of equity, caring, and respecting difference explicit. (p. 180)

The fifth element in learner-centered classrooms is the community of practice. Its intent is to demonstrate that "no one is an island; no one knows it all; cooperative learning is necessary for survival. The interdependence promotes an atmosphere of joint responsibility, mutual respect, and a sense of personal and group identity" (p. 181). The sixth and final component in a community of learners is the development of a sensitive context for learning. Each student must be developmentally and functionally challenged to his or her proximal zone of performance. The tasks must become increasingly relevant to the individual goals that the students, their parents, and their teachers determine are appropriate for them. For example, students with more severe disabilities will spend more time outside their community of learners as their needs for preparation for postschool life demand actual work experience in the community.

The Playhouse Metaphor

We have introduced the playhouse metaphor as an alternative way to think about schooling. In this metaphor, each school is a theater company expected to produce its own unique response to district and state specifications. Self-determination is expected at the student, teacher, and school level. Fostering a caring community of learners requires team learning and a sense of responsibility for the whole enterprise of learning for the community, the individual student, and the teachers. Creating learning opportunities means creating new parts and new roles for each of the actors. The play needs multiple scenes that require individual performance yet illustrate how the ensemble supports and enlarges any one individual performance. The playhouse company has multiple functions that allow all the participants to try their hands at authoring, planning, designing, arranging, constructing, painting, displaying, decorating, managing, marketing, promoting, and financing the production—in addition to performing on the stage itself. The ensemble is the metaphor for community and our individual responsibility to contribute to its well-being.

7

Organizing for
Instruction in Unified Schools

School districts across the United States have responded to demands to educate students with disabilities in regular classrooms by physically placing these students in classrooms with their age peers and providing special education teachers, aides, and related services personnel who "push in" to the classroom to provide specialized instruction. Although these efforts satisfy the need for students with disabilities to be physically proximate to their peers, they do not necessarily provide appropriate instruction, access to the general curriculum, or efficient use of instructional resources. In this chapter, we provide a framework for school organization that is necessary to merge general and special education in the classroom, school, and district to create a differentiated instructional program designed to respond to the individual needs of all students.

At Souhegan High School in Amherst, New Hampshire, the essential question is: How can schools be restructured so that the inclusion of each student in the mainstream of regular education is

113

a necessary condition for achievement of excellence by all? Souhegan's mission statement says,

> Schools of the future should strive to be communities of learners where intellectual development and adaptability to change become driving forces for everyone—students and staff alike—but where the climate is humane and caring, promoting respect for diversity. Souhegan High School aspires to be a community of learners born of respect, trust and courage. We consciously commit ourselves
>
> • To support and encourage an individual's unique gifts, passions and intentions
> • To develop and empower the mind, body and heart
> • To challenge and expand the comfortable limits of thought, tolerance and performance
> • To inspire and honor the active stewardship of family, nation and globe

Souhegan's essential question and its mission statement summarize the challenge for educators who are concerned about their efforts to meet the individual needs of students and to educate students to the higher standards that are both included in state and national reforms initiatives and necessary for an educated and productive citizenry. These efforts require that teachers think outside their classrooms and that administrators think across and outside their schools as they work to create programs and resources to meet the challenge. In addition, Souhegan has chosen to focus on the development of the student as a complete individual, a marked contrast to the rhetoric of high academic achievement that dominated educational discourse in the late 1990s. At Souhegan, education serves to support and empower, challenge, and inspire students to become members of a community that values learning.

Configuring new educational structures and working relationships will require creative thinking, learning from the practice of others, and innovative systems of professional development that encourage continuous growth and support constant change. Education has long been considered a solitary profession (Lortie, 1975) in which teachers worked in isolation—a circumstance that many educators prefer because it shields them from the outside world's intrusions. However, as calls for accountability have become more insistent and as we have learned about the power of collaborative working arrangements, the Lone Teacher, who closes the classroom door, does what she wants to do, and is solely responsible for her children's learning, has become an anachronism.

To our way of thinking, creating schools in which all students meet high standards for learning requires renewal of the concept of *integration*. For schools to be successful in providing quality and equity for all students, the disciplinary structure of curriculum must be replaced by an interdisciplinary approach that recognizes the interrelationships in knowledge. Instruction must consist of a wide variety of approaches that use enrichment, acceleration, and adaptive technologies to challenge the capacities of all students and connect their learning to their lives. Assessment must be an ongoing effort to evaluate student learning authentically and in relationship to the curriculum and instructional strategies that are in place for students. Working relationships must be interdependent to allow educators to draw upon the variety of knowledge, traditions, and skills necessary to provide challenging and motivational educational experiences for all students. School time must be organized to allow for the flexibility necessary to give all students the opportunity to express their individuality and their unique approaches to learning. Finally, supple resources must be available to provide educators the time, materials, equipment, and flexibility necessary for an education that benefits all students. Organizing schools to supply these arrangements will require that educators link interdisciplinary curriculum, interconnected instruction, interdependent relationships, authentic assessment, flexible time, and supple resources together to form an integrated approach to learning in the classroom, school, and community.

Thinking Differently
About the Nature of Education

Bringing the schools we envision to fruition will require that educators think differently about the nature of the task of educating students. Thinking differently will entail reconceptualizing our notions of learners, the learning process, knowledge, and the aims of education to bring the knowledge traditions of general and special education together in the service of learners. Reorienting educators and the institutional arrangements that support their practices means that practitioners, policymakers, and the public will have to engage in a substantive dialogue about the nature of schools in the coming years and what society needs from schools if it is to progress.

Knowledge Traditions in Education

The assumptions that support general and special education have developed from different roots in the social sciences and different aims for education. Since the passage of EHA in 1975, a dual system of education has developed in an effort to isolate those students who cannot function successfully in the dominant general education program. Special education has developed as a rationalist and objectivist parallel system, the purpose of which is to contain the problem of failure in public schools (Skrtic, 1991). Practices; understandings of students, teaching, and learning; and organizational approaches to instruction and assessment differ substantively in the dual systems of general and special education.

The knowledge tradition in general education emphasizes developing a substantive scope and sequence in curriculum, delivering curriculum to groups of students, and using standardized assessments to evaluate student progress. Implementing high standards, the current approach to improving educational outcomes, addresses each of these components by developing standards in each curricular area, creating new models for grouping, and regularly monitoring student progress through comprehensive testing programs. The preparation of general education teachers, in addition to structuring the learning environment, includes areas such as content knowledge, curriculum objectives, curriculum materials, content resources support, content development, and curriculum sequence (White & White, 1992).

The knowledge tradition in special education emphasizes adapting curriculum, individualizing curriculum and instruction, motivating students who have difficulty learning independently, and assessing progress toward individually established learning goals.

Improving special education and the responsiveness of schools to the individual needs of students has focused on providing an array of service configurations for small groups of students, adapting the general curriculum to provide that which is essential for these students, and using assessment data to plan appropriate instructional programs. The preparation of special education teachers includes areas such as knowledge of disabilities, individual learning styles, adaptation of curriculum, learning strategies, modifications to the learning environment, legal issues, and motivational techniques (White & White, 1992).

As the need to educate all children to high standards has received attention in the political rhetoric surrounding education, many researchers and policymakers have recognized that the dual system should be merged if schools are to provide improved opportunities for all students. To merge services effectively and create classrooms that meet the individual needs of all students, the two knowledge traditions must be merged and synthesized to make the knowledge, skills, and dispositions of each tradition available to the instructional problem-solving efforts of each teacher and to invent new knowledge that enables teachers to transform their practices. Creating classrooms that effectively and appropriately include all students will require that the preservice preparation and professional development of all teachers include understanding shared teaching, evaluation, classroom management, student supervision, team problem solving, communication skills, responses to change, addressing social and emotional needs, and the absolute necessity of ongoing professional growth.

Conceptualizing a Paradigm Shift in Curriculum, Instruction, and Assessment

Elkind (1989) has conceptualized the discourse on teaching and learning into two paradigms of practice: the psychometric approach and the developmentally appropriate approach. Elkind's notions are useful because they help us see the contrasts in our thinking about learners, the learning process, knowledge, and the aims of education. The knowledge traditions of general and special education are rooted in a psychometric understanding of learners, which special education has taken to an extreme in the behaviorist and objectivist discourse that has been dominant in special education (Skrtic, 1991).

Whereas the psychometric approach continues to dominate policymaking and accountability initiatives, most educators recognize that a different approach is at work in their classrooms. As a result, they are forced to accommodate their practical understandings of the developmentally appropriate practice paradigm to fit the demands of state and federal decision makers for measurable outcomes. Educators have not been particularly good at debunking the myths that are foisted upon them by the psychometric dominance of policymaking, and they have a difficult job ahead of them to convince themselves, policymakers, and the public that more differentiated ways of thinking about learners and learning are necessary to respond to the needs of the increasingly diverse student populations in our schools at the turn of the 21st century.

Psychometric Practice: Conceptions of Learners, the Learning Process, Knowledge, and the Aims of Education

The psychometric paradigm (Elkind, 1989) of educational practice argues that learners' abilities are quantifiable and that schools are society's agents for sorting and selecting students according to their abilities. Knowledge is a set of skills and dispositions that a student acquires through education, and the degree to which a student has acquired knowledge can be measured against the master list of skills and dispositions that were intended to be acquired. How students learn and the content they learn are not connected, and, as a result, students' thinking and interactions with the world around them occur independent of context. Knowledge is a real list of skills and dispositions to be acquired; its acquisition can be measured objectively; and the content of knowledge and the process of learning are not related. The purpose of the educational system, then, is to ensure that students have acquired as much of a body of knowledge as possible and to certify those students who have acquired more knowledge than others, so that the most meritorious learners can assume important positions in society.

The psychometric paradigm dominated educational thinking throughout the 20th century. Its influence was evident in the 1990s in the push for high standards of student achievement and high-stakes testing. For example, in North Carolina, which has been hailed by political leaders as a bastion of sound educational practice (see President Clinton's 1999 State of the Union Address and Secretary of Education Richard Riley's 1999 State of Education Address), the State Board of Education has stipulated the curriculum in all North Carolina public schools through its passage of the standard course of study, in which the knowledge students should acquire is detailed for teachers. Students are then tested annually on the content of the standard course of study through end-of-grade and end-of-course examinations. Students who do not pass these tests must participate in remedial activities, usually in the form of summer school, and show passing progress to move to the next grade. Teachers and administrators are held accountable for student progress and receive merit pay if 80% of the students in a school progress at the state-prescribed rate. Although teachers and administrators still have some discretion about moving students along if they do not show mastery, President Clinton's admonitions about social promotion and Governor Hunt's proposals to eliminate it cast the specter of students who cannot pass tests stuck in grade for years at a time.

The psychometric paradigm is foundational to the special education knowledge tradition, which Skrtic (1991) places in the extreme objectivist sector of functionalist thought. As we all know, eligibility for special education is based primarily on a student's performance on standardized measures of intelligence and achievement. In the case of special education, the body of knowledge for which the student is held accountable is the curriculum loosely defined by the test authors and the norming process. Tests of intelligence purport to measure a student's ability to learn independent of content and, as a result a student's performance on abstract tasks such as block design and picture arrangement, are used as indicators of that student's ability to learn. If a student is judged to be sufficiently defective to require special education, then an allegedly unique curriculum, documented by the IEP, is devised for him. Student progress and prospective return to the regular classroom are determined by his acquisition of the knowledge, skills, and dispositions indicated on the IEP. For students with disabilities, this process performs the ultimate sorting and selecting function that is justified by its putative objectivity, and it shields the school from being responsible for the student's progress. Efforts to provide access to the regular education curriculum (IDEA, 1997) to the contrary, many schools and districts have used placement in special education as a means to bracket the test scores of poorly achieving students and thereby avoid account-ability for their progress.

Many educators understand the problems that are associated with the psychometric paradigm, but their perspective is warped by their own grounding in its assumptions and by the power of the paradigm as evidenced in its acceptance by legislators and highly visible education advocates from the business community. As a result, educators often turn to positions that advocate for tinkering with the paradigm at its margins. Creating better tests, reorganizing the curriculum, or providing special services for students who fail are three efforts that arise out of educators' dissatisfaction with the assumptions of the psychometric paradigm and the policies resulting from them. Because they are products of the psychometric paradigm, many educators are unprepared to look at a paradigm of practice based on assumptions that are more in line with educational purposes that value all students equally and foster differentiated learning and instruction.

Developmentally Appropriate Practice:
Conceptions of Learners, the Learning Process,
Knowledge, and the Aims of Education

Elkind (1989) offers a paradigm of developmentally appropriate practice, the assumptions of which are in stark contrast to the psychometric paradigm. Programs that match the assumptions of the developmentally appropriate practice are more responsive to the needs of diverse learners and provide the knowledge, skills, and dispositions that are necessary for economic productivity and social participation at the turn of the century. Under the assumptions of developmentally appropriate practice, learners are constant works in progress who develop their knowledge, skills, and dispositions as they interact with the world around them. As a result, each learner learns differently as she creates meaning from her experiences. Learners are most effective when they are engaged in creative and constructive activities that capitalize on their emerging abilities. The purpose of education is to provide the opportunity for learners to engage in knowledge creation, to foster the development of creativity and critical thinking, and to build habits of lifelong learning. In this paradigm, the content and processes of learning are inextricably linked. Each student progresses differently, and learning is meaning making. Students have a natural inclination to learn, and they learn especially well when they participate in rich educational environments. Measuring student progress through standardized assessments is neither useful nor practical. Because students learn differently, tests do not give a true picture of their achievement; because learning is meaning making, the only assessments that make sense are those in which the student is asked to perform an authentic task.

Educators are confounded by the concepts that constitute the developmentally appropriate practice model. Although they might recognize the inherent sensibility of the philosophical construction of the model, they do not have the knowledge and skills necessary to create classrooms that are organized within those philosophical boundaries, and they are constantly faced with the pressures and demands brought on by the dominance of the psychometric model in policymaking circles. One contribution of the legal pressure to include students with disabilities in general education classrooms and schools is that educators are also faced with pressures and demands to differentiate their educational environments and instructional programs. Whereas many throw up their hands in frustration at these dual stressors, others have taken the opportunity to examine their practices and to create new educational approaches that fit their professional values and accommodate policy demands.

Our thinking about schools calls for adoption of the assumptions of a developmentally appropriate practice paradigm, and we believe that special educators can play an important role in bringing the shift about, even though their own practices will be the most radically changed. Special education has played an important role in education by allowing teachers and administrators to experiment with variations in curriculum, instruction, and assessment. We submit that efforts to merge general and special education present the opportunity to play the experimental role again.

Demands to include students with disabilities raise important questions, which can become a basis for transforming educational practice. However, transforming educational practices requires not only changing the structures and cultural patterns of schools; more important, transforming schools requires a shift in how we think about learners, the learning process, knowledge, and the aims of education. To our way of thinking, learners are actively engaged in constructing new knowledge that helps them make sense of the world around them. The purpose of education is to support and empower, challenge, and inspire all learners to become members of a community that understands that learning is the key to the good life. Since our notions center around the idea that all students should be a part of that learning community, we are especially concerned with how schools will organize themselves into a unified system that supports the learning community and how students with disabilities and other special needs come to be included in the community.

Educational Collaboration

Unifying special and general education programs entails changing the nature of work relationships and instructional interactions of the faculty, staff, and administration. Innovations in the private sector suggest that collaborative arrangements provide solutions to the problems that arise when work consists of complex tasks, such as teaching and learning. In this section, we describe collaboration as a means of addressing the needs of all students in unified schools and classrooms and to improving the work life and morale of school personnel.

Collaboration, as we use it, includes a number of approaches in which power, responsibility, and accountability are shared among the various constituencies that are charged with the task of educating all students in a learning community. Collaborative arrangements have been used in innovative approaches to governance, curriculum development, professional development, and instruction with some degree of success. In many cases, the charge to share responsibility in education has been mandated through top-down directives, and as a result these efforts have met with resistance from the grassroots people who have to implement activities they do not understand or support.

Collaboration entails a commitment to democratic principles that require levels of openness, discourse, and change that make those who have power and those who have been accustomed to implementing directives uncomfortable. Engaging in democratic work relationships is hard work; democracy is not characterized by tidiness, routine, or efficiency. School personnel are accustomed to working in a professional bureaucracy that values order, efficiency, and routinization of educational tasks. Any effort to change decision making or work relationships requires intensive discussion, training, and reeducation for all persons who will be involved in collaborative approaches, but learning to function as a collaborator in a democratic school is integral to working in a school that transmits democratic values to students through the thoughts and actions of the adults in a learning community.

Collaborative Governance

Collaboration as an approach to governance has taken many forms, but its essence entails inviting the constituencies who are affected by decisions to be involved in the decision-making process, the implementation, and the evaluation of and accountability for decisions. Collaborative governance entails (a) forming representative teams, (b) charging the teams with decision-making responsibilities, (c) establishing a decision-making process, and (d) monitoring the implementation of decisions to determine their effectiveness and to plan next steps. New York's *A New Compact for Learning* (1992) is an excellent example of the effort to share decision making among boards of education, administrators, teachers, parents, and community members. Implementation of the *Compact* is also a study in the difficulties that arise from attempting to implement shared decision making in schools and districts.

Forming Representative Teams. The membership of representative teams is generally stipulated in the policy that governs collaborative decision making. Membership often depends on the nature of the decisions the teams are intended to make and the degree to which governance is to be democratically shared. Typically, teams charged with educational responsibility consist of administrators, teachers, parents, and nonparent community members, although nonprofessional school personnel and students are sometimes also included. In New York, each school district was required to form a district-wide *Compact* committee that minimally consisted of administrators, teachers, and parents. Subsequently, schools were also required to form a school-shared decision-making team that would make recommendations to the district administration and board of education about the operation of the school. Principals, teachers, and parents comprised these school-based teams.

Controversies abound over the membership of shared decision-making teams. In some cases, teams of teachers are charged with the responsibility to make decisions that affect the curricular, instructional, and assessment programs in the school—responsibilities that have traditionally resided with administrators and often in the district office. In other situations, parents become involved in decisions that have traditionally been the province of administrators and teachers, such as choosing textbooks and instructional materials, reviewing school assessment results, or organizing the school's schedule. In any case, shared decision making is intended to broaden participation in educational governance in an effort to involve those who are responsible for ensuring that the decisions have the results intended and to increase support for decisions. If students are to become active in constructing knowledge and determining their educational futures, they must see shared decision making in action in their schools.

Decision-Making Responsibilities. Shared decision-making policies usually stipulate the kinds of decisions that representative teams are empowered to make and the process by which their deliberations occur. The nature of the decisions that are entrusted to shared decision making is a significant indicator of the seriousness given to the importance of the process. In some states and districts, shared governance teams are empowered to make significant decisions about curriculum, personnel, and allocation of resources. When the teams' deliberations include issues that have a direct, observable influence on the educational status of students or the working conditions of personnel, teams are more likely to take their roles and their power seriously. However, when the discussions at meetings and the decisions they make appear trivial, interest is likely to decline precipitously. How much power and impact-shared decision making teams have is a function of the willingness of policymakers (such as board members) and administrators to let go of their authority in order to enable other stakeholders to exercise power. Because theories of shared decision making are rooted in democracy and because democracy is often slow and inefficient, policymakers and administrators are often hesitant to give up their discretion over issues of significance in schools. As a result, shared governance has often been viewed by stakeholder-participants as a sham in which upper-level policymakers and administrators pay lip service to empowerment but do little to distribute authority over issues and resources that can make a difference in the classrooms and schools.

Policies also generally stipulate the authority of shared governance teams and the weight of their decisions. Whether the teams' decisions function as advice, recommendations, or requirements influences the teams' responses. Teams whose actions are advisory may view their roles to be superfluous and, as a result, make pie-in-the-sky proposals, or conversely, not take their roles seriously. Teams whose decisions become requirements may usurp legal or constitutional responsibilities of administrators or boards of education. In most cases, shared governance teams' decisions are couched as recommendations, which administrators or boards must take into account as they make the decisions for which they are responsible.

Decision-Making Processes. The process that shared-governance teams use as they consider courses of action can vary widely. Some factors that influence the process are the mode of agreement required, the time, and the commitment of team members. The mode of agreement used in decision making refers to the kind of consent necessary for a decision to move forward. Some efforts have been made to make decisions by pure consensus—that is, every member of the team must agree with the proposed course of action and pledge to support it publicly. Such unanimity is hard to come by, especially with difficult, complex educational issues. As a result, teams can come to the point where they reach consensus on matters that are so general or so vague that they are meaningless, and this sense creates frustration and destroys the morale of team members. However, when teams can come to consensus on matters of substance, the likelihood that important progress will be made is significantly enhanced.

Other shared governance processes are based on some form of majority rule—a simple majority (50% + one vote) or a supermajority (60%, $\frac{2}{3}$, or $\frac{3}{4}$). Majority rule has its advantages: It is easier to gain a majority than it is to gain consensus; therefore moving forward is more likely to occur expeditiously. However, majority rule also leaves open the possibility that a significant number of dissenters exist who can stall or block implementation of a decision.

An advantage to unilateral decision making has been that decisions can be made quickly. Shared governance requires more time.

The process of making a decision requires convening meetings, giving members the opportunity for deliberation, and allowing for a consensus or majority to develop about the course of action that should be taken. All of these prolong the decision-making process, which can cause difficulties for the school and frustrate those who are looking for fast action.

Commitment of team members is also a significant factor in shared governance. Team members must commit time and energy to shared governance and they must be committed to staying the course through the frustration that can accrue because of the process. Team members should have a shared vision of what they want the school to be and how their shared understandings are enacted in the decisions they make. Having participated in democratic decision making gives teachers an understanding of what must be done to include students in the vision for the school and to help them establish their own visions for their educational lives.

Monitoring Progress. Inasmuch as the shared governance team is responsible for making decisions about the school's future, it must also have a role in ensuring that its decisions are implemented as planned and in making course corrections that arise as a result of unanticipated consequences or changes in the social environment. To accomplish these tasks, school teams must view school renewal as an ongoing process of growth and development that requires a continual commitment to improvement. Change in schools has often been understood as an incident in which structures and practices are changed to create improvement. We have learned that improving schools requires an ongoing commitment to organizational learning and renewal (Fullen, 1995; Senge, 1990). Rather than understanding what happens after a decision is made as follow-up, school teams must be designed to continue their work of reviewing, discussing, and renewing efforts to make schools better.

Schools that engage teachers, parents, and community members in activities that help determine the future have taken a first step toward educational democracy. As adults learn the lessons of their own participation, they become better able to teach students about the freedoms and responsibilities that accrue to those who live in a democracy.

Curriculum Development and Professional Development

Implementing shared governance and other changes in the politics of schools have prompted some schools to institute collaborative approaches to curriculum development and professional development. The rationale for these initiatives is the same as that for shared governance generally: Those who are most affected by decisions should have a hand in crafting alternatives and deciding on courses of action. However, there is another force at work in curriculum and professional development that has a marked influence on how decisions are made—accountability. Because schools and the public are more concerned about the outcomes and productivity of schools, schools have had to respond to concerns about their effectiveness by including teachers, parents, students, and community members in decision making.

The impetus for broadening the base of decision making in curriculum comes from two sources: (a) teachers, who need to understand the curricular demands that are made on their students and (b) parents and political activists, who are concerned about encroachment of the schools into areas of learning that have traditionally been within the purview of the family or church. Teachers are particularly concerned about the curriculum because of the high stakes that have been attached to testing programs. Because most states and districts have done a credible job aligning statewide evaluations with prescribed curriculum, teachers are very serious about any decision regarding textbooks, instructional materials, or additional content. Teachers are concerned that they know what is expected in the curriculum and subsequently on tests, how instructional materials will help their students reach expected standards, how new or different content will support their efforts to ensure that students score well on standardized tests, and how they will pack all the demands that are made into a finite amount of instructional time.

Parents and political activists have challenged the curriculum in a variety of instances. Sexuality education content, HIV/AIDS curriculum, literature selections, outcomes-based education, and the availability of books in the school library are some of the areas that have been objects of controversy between schools and parents. When these issues have been litigated, the courts have generally ruled that schools have discretion over curricular decisions, if they have a policy about how such decisions are made and if they follow their policy. As a result, schools have developed policies that give committees of teachers and parents the opportunity to review curriculum, textbooks, instructional materials, and library holdings to gain their input about the suitability of these items for use in the school. When these committees make their recommendations, the school is on safe ground against challenges because it can appeal to its policy of consulting with teachers and parents before curricular decisions are made (McCarthy, Cambron-McCabe, & Thomas, 1998).

In the area of professional development, teachers have expressed an interest in participating in decision making because they see this area as particularly important to their work lives. Many schools and districts have staff development councils that devise professional development programs, grant continuing education credit, and align professional development with the instructional goals and other regulatory demands that are made by state and federal educational agencies. As demands for instructional accountability have increased, teachers have recognized the need to be more aware of and skilled at working with the demands of curriculum, assessment, and accountability systems. As a result, they are most interested in the design of professional development programs that are germane to their jobs, provide practical help in meeting job demands, and help them develop networks of support with others teachers.

Using learning-centered leadership, teachers who participate in the governance, curriculum, and professional development processes can move their schools toward becoming learning organizations (Senge, 1990). As they organize themselves for democratic participation, they model democratic processes for students and begin to see the broader interests that affect schools. The challenge of democratic participation in schools are twofold: (a) organizing governance, curriculum, and professional development as ongoing, discursive processes that value organizational learning and (b) ensuring that all those who are affected by decisions have a voice in the conversation about the nature of the school. Since our interest in the current project is ensuring that students with disabilities are adequately represented in the school-community conversation, we now turn to a framework for the school's discussion about including students with disabilities in all the schools' functions, operations, and responsibilities.

Including Students
With Disabilities in Regular Classrooms

Questions and Implications

As we consider the placement of students with disabilities in regular schools and general education classrooms, there are some important questions that must be addressed by teachers and administrators. These questions raise important issues related to students' needs, provision of services, and instructional strategies. The questions are drawn from Skrtic's (1991) seminal work in which he looks behind special education at the assumptions that have historically supported special education practice. We suggest that a team of school personnel begin the conversation about including students with disabilities in the school and that the team broaden the discourse to encompass the entire school community. As the discourse proceeds, we argue that it becomes a consideration of issues of learning diversity that encompasses all students whom schools have historically failed.

Which Students With Disabilities
Will Be Included?

Although decisions regarding the placement of students with disabilities are made on an individual basis, there are some important considerations that must be addressed as the team that is planning for inclusive practice creates the model that will be used in the school. First, some discussion must occur about the purposes of inclusive placement. Students with disabilities are placed in regular classrooms for a variety of reasons: to improve their educational achievement, to improve their social adjustment, to create heterogeneous classrooms, to experiment with new teacher work arrangements. Knowing the purposes being pursued and how they fit with the school's posture toward excellence and equity are important considerations in the approaches taken to include students with disabilities in the school.

In the beginning, some decisions will have to be made about which students will be included and which personnel will work with them. How those decisions are made have significant implications for planning, teacher training, instructional and assessment accommodations, scheduling, and working relationships, as well as the legal exposure of the school district. Obviously, these decisions must be made within the confines of the IEP and due process of law.

Some school districts have chosen to begin their inclusive programs by placing students with severe disabilities in the regular classroom with the special education teacher and other support personnel providing a parallel curriculum for the student. The student participates in class social interactions and, to a limited extent, in class academic activities. The purpose of the placement in these cases is to provide a socialization experience for both the student with disabilities and his typical peers and to meet his instructional needs through direct instruction by the special education teacher and peer tutoring and interactions. This approach has the advantage of opening the regular classroom door to students with disabilities. However, it does not require very much in the way of accommodation to the curriculum or instructional strategies that are already in place in the regular classroom teacher's repertoire.

Other school districts have begun their inclusive efforts by increasing the amount of time students with disabilities spend in the regular classroom and changing the roles and functions of the special education teacher from disciplinary specialist to consulting or collaborating teacher. Generally, the students with disabilities who are included under this model are those whose educational expectations are the same as those for the typical students in the classroom, that is, students with mild disabilities who are expected to read, write, do math, and perform in the content areas. The success of this approach often rests on the compatibility of the teachers who are working together and keeping the number of students with disabilities for whom they are responsible reasonable. A variation on this scheme is combining a special education class of 10 students with a general education class of about the same number and having the two teachers collaborate. Typically, this arrangement is not successful, especially when the general education students are chosen because they have academic difficulties.

Which Services Will Be Merged?

Successfully including students with disabilities in regular schools and classrooms requires that new forms of service delivery be developed. Considerable work has been done in areas such as collaboration and co-teaching (which are discussed in the next chapter), and many special educators hope for the day when other teachers and administrators will have the expertise and the proper disposition about supporting students with disabilities. Though developing new models of service is important, it is also important to attach meaning to the work of those who educate these students and to attune everyone to the philosophical and social thinking that undergirds the movement to include students. The assumptions and motives that are inherent in successful inclusive practice are sometimes at odds with the assumptions and motives that are traditional in schools and classrooms.

Administrators who are creating models for successful inclusion are becoming increasingly aware that collaboration is an important tool for breaking the culture of isolated work that pervades schools. Creating the time for collaborative planning, training, and instruction are important components of any inclusive program, and time is often the most difficult resource to arrange, especially because arranging for personnel time requires money. Teachers who work together must have time to get to know one another as individuals and professionals and to develop the instructional repertoire they will use with students. Once their relationship has been established, more practical questions, such as who is responsible for which instruction and how evaluative judgments will be made, can be addressed.

As teachers develop their collaborative relationships, they must address issues of practice that are fundamental to their understanding of teaching. Teachers who work together must determine how they will structure the classroom, which instructional methods are mutually agreeable, how curriculum will be determined, and how student behavior will be managed. Many schools have begun to implement interdisciplinary teaming and curriculum, cross-age grouping, and looping, which further blur the traditional lines that teachers have drawn to circumscribe their work. In schools where time is at a premium, these demands may seem insurmountable. Although all these decisions must be made by individual teachers in their work, the act of sharing the decisions makes them infinitely more complex, since two minds, personalities, sets of habits, and idiosyncrasies are at work in the decision-making process and these decisions affect that which is thought to be most sacred in professional education—the sanctity of the classroom. Stretching curricular and instructional boundaries has many advantages for all students, but it makes the work of teachers more complicated and requires more time for thought, planning, and action.

The administrative challenge in creating successful inclusive models is to provide time, resources, training, experience, and leadership to support collaborative teaching relationships. Collaborative teaching can be linked to shared governance, multidisciplinary curriculum, and interdisciplinary teaming to form a package of cooperative strategies that change the culture of the school. These changes require school leaders to articulate the philosophical and logistical perspectives necessary to raise awareness about what the school is trying to accomplish and to build support for school activities. In a time of high-stakes accountability, school leaders must be able to show that the innovations they advocate will result in improved outcomes for all students. It is often said that improving achievement test scores in a school is really a function of improving the instructional status of students in the lower quartiles. School change initiatives should focus on strategies that raise achievement for these students, while also enriching the learning experiences of all students.

Which Instructional Technologies Will Be Supported?

Including students with disabilities in general education classrooms requires that teachers adopt instructional strategies and use instructional technologies that are aligned with learning-centered principles. Examples of these strategies and technologies are discussed in the next chapter. However, merely adopting new strategies and technologies is a necessary but insufficient aspect of the process of instructional change. Before teachers change their classroom practice, they must be involved in discourse, program development, and training that prepare them and the school-community for their new approaches. We suggest that a yearlong discussion of the purposes of inclusive practice, the approaches that will be used, and their implications for the education of all students occur and that administrators, teachers, parents, members of the community, and, in some cases, students participate. Questions such as these must be discussed broadly, for the issues they raise are critical to the success of inclusive practice and to the dialogue on improving schools for all students:

1. How will time, resources, training, experience, and leadership be provided to support cooperative learning, curriculum-based assessment, peer tutoring, adaptive learning, and individualized instruction?
2. Will curricular adaptations and expectations for student learning be compatible?
3. Will student and teacher evaluation systems support curricular and instructional accommodations?
4. How will efforts to adapt curriculum and instruction affect currently used assessment systems? How will currently used assessment systems affect curricular and instructional adaptations?

Summary

The schools we envision operate democratically to model democratic practices for students and to ensure that the purposes, processes, and aspirations of all members of the school community are considered as schooling proceeds. Democratic schooling requires new ways of thinking about curriculum, instruction, assessment, and working relationships, and it entails an ongoing community discourse about the nature of schooling. Bringing together the knowledge traditions of general and special education can provide a vehicle for this discourse, and special educators can play a critical role in shaping the conversation so that issues of diversity and differentiation are constantly being considered.

In the next chapter, we discuss a number of instructional and curricular alternatives that can be used to educate students with disabilities in general education schools and classrooms. The revisions of IDEA 97 stipulate that students with disabilities have access to the general education curriculum, that they must participate in statewide assessments, and that their progress in the general curriculum be reported on regularly. Schools that are organized democratically will need strategies and tactics to meet these requirements, which are intended to ensure that the needs of students with disabilities remain at the forefront of educational decision making. Our next chapter provides some guidance for school personnel interested in proceeding with inclusive practice.

8

Delivering Instruction in Unified Schools

Our vision of unified schools embraces the notion that the school's responsibility is to meet the diverse academic, social, and emotional needs of all students. To accomplish this task, schools must assert themselves as academic and social centers that represent the interests of children. Although they will not replace the family, church, and community as institutions responsible for the acculturation of children, schools should step in to fill the gaps created when the capacities of social institutions change to children's detriment. This new role will require that schools become community centers in which resources for learning, care, health, and nurturance are made available when children need them.

Our vision of schooling also contains a revival of the school's role as a community center for personal growth and social support. Schools have resources for learning, facilities, technologies, and expertise that can be useful in fulfilling the educational, economic, social, and recreational needs of all members of the community. In our view, the school should serve as a social and educational hub around which a community organizes itself for the betterment of its diverse citizenry.

If schools are to meet the challenges that our vision describes, they must be organized in new ways, and they must conduct the business of learning differently. In other chapters, we have discussed the work of Senge (1990), in which he details the workings of learning organizations. It may seem odd to say that schools must become learning organizations; after all, isn't learning what they are organized to convey to students? However, schools as they are currently organized are not learning organizations in Senge's sense. Instead, they are organized as professional bureaucracies (Skrtic, 1991) that deliver a product called education. The schools we envision will need to be organized to create new solutions to the problems that arise when diverse groups of learners make academic, social, and emotional demands related to the school's dual missions—meeting the needs of all learners and serving as an educational and social resource to the community.

Creating unified schools as learning organizations entails using new forms of school organization, flexible time arrangements, collaborative personnel patterns, adaptable instructional approaches, an emerging curriculum, versatile and authentic assessments, and shared accountability. We have had the privilege to encounter schools that have organized themselves to respond quickly and effectively to the dynamic educational needs of diverse students. In these schools, we have seen new sets of assumptions about the nature of learning and learners. These assumptions are best described by learner-centered psychological principles, which have been described by McCombs and Whisler (1997), and it is to a delineation of these principles that we now turn.

Learner-Centered Psychological Principles

In an effort to provide guidance about the contribution the field of psychology might make to improving schools, the American Psychological Association commissioned a series of studies "to integrate, from psychology, education, and related disciplines, research and theory concerned with education and the process of schooling" (McCombs & Whisler, 1997, p. 3). From these studies emerged the learner-centered psychological principles and a definition of learner-centered:

> The perspective that couples a focus on individual learners (their hereditary, experiences, perspectives, backgrounds, talents, interests, capacities, and needs) with a focus on learning (the best available knowledge about learning and how it occurs and about teaching practices that are most effective in promoting the highest levels of motivation, learning, and achievement for all learners). This dual focus then informs and drives educational decision making. The learner-centered perspective is a reflection of the twelve learner-centered psychological principles in the programs, practices, policies, and people that support learning for all. (p. 9)

From this definition and the learner-centered psychological principles, McCombs and Whisler (1997) have distilled five premises of the learner-centered model:

1. Learners are distinct and unique. Their distinctiveness and uniqueness must be attended to and taken into account if learners are to engage in and take responsibility for their own learning.
2. Learners' unique differences include their emotional states of mind, learning rates, learning styles, stages of development, abilities, talents, feelings of efficacy, and other academic and nonacademic attributes and needs. These must be taken into account if all learners are to be provided with the necessary challenges and opportunities for learning and self-development.
3. Learning is a constructive process that occurs best when what is being learned is relevant and meaningful to the learner and when the learner is actively engaged in creating his or her own knowledge and understanding by connecting what is being learned with prior knowledge and experience.
4. Learning occurs best in a positive environment that contains comfort and order, and positive interpersonal relationships and interactions, in which the learner feels appreciated, acknowledged, respected, and validated.

5. Learning is a fundamentally natural process; learners are naturally curious and basically interested in learning about and mastering their world. Although negative thoughts and feelings sometimes interfere with this natural inclination and must be dealt with, the learner does not require "fixing." (p. 10)

The learner-centered psychological principles and our interpretations of their meaning for schools are summarized in Table 8.1. We believe that these principles serve as the philosophical and psychological foundation for schools that merge services for supporting all students in their learning in a unified school. Delivering instruction in learning-centered schools, then, entails choosing instructional methods, approaches, curriculum, and assessment techniques that try to connect learning to students' search for meaning in their environments and in their lives. Although they all want to learn, each student brings a unique perspective to the learning experience, which has not always been valued or successful. Teachers are responsible for helping students learn how to learn and how to think. Acknowledging and celebrating individual differences encourages learning because students learn best when they understand that they are cared for and respected. Still, students learn differently, and their experience must be the cornerstone on which additional learning is built. This requires instructional approaches that recognize the variety of rates and styles of learning that drive students' understanding of the academic, social, and emotional worlds in which they live.

In the remainder of this chapter, we discuss a variety of instructional approaches used in schools and classrooms that include students with disabilities. These approaches represent the contribution of the knowledge tradition of special education to the merger of general and special education instructional strategies that we propose.

Adapting Curriculum and Instruction in Inclusive Classrooms

The Center for School-Community Integration (CSCI) in the Institute for Disability and Community at Indiana University has developed an in-service training package and videotape that depicts nine dimensions of adapting curriculum and instruction. We have used

TABLE 8.1

Educational Implications and Practices Related to
Learner-Centered Psychological Principles

Learner-Centered Psychological Principles	Educational Implications
1. Nature of the learning process	1. Everyone wants to learn, if the learning means something to him or her personally.
2. Goals of the learning process	2. Learning occurs most successfully when students place new knowledge into some context they already understand and care about.
3. Construction of knowledge	3. Learning occurs most successfully when what students already know, what they need to know, and the relevance of the learning to their life are linked together in the learning experience.
4. Higher-order thinking	4. Teachers need to help students identify and develop their personal "thinking about thinking" strategies.
5. Motivational influences on learning	5. Readiness to learn is affected by individual differences, self-image, and the individual's emotional state.
6. Intrinsic motivation to learn	6. Children are naturally enthusiastic about learning; however, negative feedback can destroy this innate tendency.
7. Characteristics of motivation-enhancing learning tasks	7. Curiosity, creativity, and problem solving are motivated by learning experiences that include activities that have personal meaning for students.
8. Developmental constraints and opportunities	8. Learning occurs most successfully when teachers use developmentally appropriate materials that acknowledge differences in physical, intellectual, emotional, and social areas of development.

(Continued)

TABLE 8.1
(Continued)

Learner-Centered Psychological Principles	Educational Implications
9. Social and cultural diversity	9. Learning occurs most successfully when individual differences, backgrounds, and cultures are respected.
10. Social acceptance, self-esteem, and learning	10. Students will respond positively to any individual they believe sincerely cares about them personally and who values the students' unique interests and talents.
11. Individual differences in learning	11. Although all children can learn, they do so at different rates using different styles.
12. Cognitive filters	12. Students' experiences shape their understanding of their world and drive their learning.

this package extensively with audiences of general and special education teachers at all grade levels and have found it an excellent vehicle for raising awareness of the issues inherent in inclusive classrooms and for providing skills that teachers need to respond to the needs of all students.

In our sessions with teachers, we begin with a discussion of the assumptions that undergird our support of instructional practice for diverse learners. Ebeling, Deschenes, and Sprague (1994) provide guidance for this discussion by listing these assumptions:

1. Adapting is for all students.
2. Adapting is not new.
3. Adapting is best approached through collaborative problem solving.
4. Adapting starts with individual student goals.
5. Adapting maximizes participation in typical curriculum and instruction.
6. Adapting can be supported by instructional strategies. (pp. 4-5)

This discussion helps teachers understand that much of what is required for their efforts to include students with special learning needs is (a) good practice for all students, (b) familiar to them as good practice, and (c) a collaborative process that will support them in solving instructional problems. This discussion sets the stage for broaching collaboration, differentiated instruction, high expectations for all students, and methods of assessing student work, all of which are unfamiliar to many teachers and which raise their stress level. By assuring teachers that they have many of the skills they need to educate all students in the classrooms, we begin to build on their current knowledge of best practice and provide them support for meeting high standards and accountability measures for all students. As we link inclusive practice to solving other problems about which teachers are concerned, we are building the foundation for changes that alter the pedagogical core of schools.

Adapting curriculum and instruction necessitates a discussion about the purposes and structure of curriculum, its content, methods of instruction, and the purposes and structure of assessments used in the school, district, and state. We find that many teachers have never engaged in this discussion. Too often teachers have taken for granted the nature of the curriculum that has been passed down to them. They have adopted the most efficient, but not necessarily effective, instructional approaches they can identify because of the pressure they feel to cover the designated curriculum before the almighty tests must be given. Rarely have teachers engaged in a prolonged discussion of whether what they teach is important for students (a crucial first step to communicating its importance to students) or what they might do to teach it more effectively. Inherent in this discussion is consideration of what instructional effectiveness means in the school and community.

We use this dialogue to encourage teachers to think that effectiveness in instruction means that all students accomplish valued outcomes that are appropriate to preparing them for the rest of their lives. Meeting this definition of instructional effectiveness requires adaptations to the curriculum and instruction that both meets the needs of students and extends learning. In concert with cross-school discourse about adapting curriculum and instruction, teachers must also analyze and critically reflect on the curriculum and standards they are expected to teach and reach some agreement about what these mean for all students. There are two crucial questions for this discussion: How can instruction be delivered so that advanced students, typical students, struggling students, poor students, students for whom English is a second language, students with mild disabilities, and students with significant disabilities can meet or exceed high standards? What can school do to provide support for teachers as they work with the diverse students they have before them?

Table 8.2 describes the types of curricular and instructional adaptations, the questions we raise in training, and some examples that have been provided by teachers as means to implement these approaches. We have found that teachers recognize that adapting simply entails using the best practices to which they have been introduced in other sessions they have attended that were geared toward improving instruction. Their greatest concern comes from the imposition of curriculum standards and high-stakes assessment and the pressure they feel to cover the required content to prepare students to perform well on standardized tests. The discussion of particular types of adaptations also opens the floor for consideration of testing practices, grading, the use of instructional aides, the nature of teacher collaboration, and the degree to which teachers perceive that standards can be made applicable to the education of all students.

As a final step in our training of teachers to include students with disabilities in regular classrooms, we take them through a series of steps for adapting curriculum and instruction (Ebeling et al., 1994). This process is most successful when teachers think critically about what they are trying to accomplish in a particular lesson, how it relates to the standards they want students to achieve, and how they can adapt their approach to meet the needs of all students. As they get better at this process, they come to understand that adapting the curriculum is a reflection of their creativity and intelligence as teachers and that it improves the likelihood that all students will meet expectations. These are the steps in adapting instruction:

1. Select the subject area to be taught.
2. Select the topic to be taught.
3. Briefly identify the curricular goal for most learners.
4. Briefly identify the instructional plan for most learners.
5. Identify learners who will need adaptations in the curriculum or instructional plan.
6. Based on individual learner goals, choose an appropriate mix of adaptations, beginning with the least intrusive.

TABLE 8.2
Curricular and Instructional Adaptations

Types of Adaptations	Questions to Ask	Examples/Opportunities for Discussion
Input	How are content and instruction delivered to the student?	Books on tape, notetakers, cooperative learning, peer tutoring, active learning
Output	How will the student demonstrate knowledge?	Projects, oral presentations, peer tutoring, multiple intelligences
Scope	Must every student learn every component or meet every objective?	Reduced assignments, differentiated grading, essential curriculum
Difficulty	Can the level of the lesson be adapted?	Functional vocabulary, use of calculators, high-interest and low-vocabulary materials
Level of support	What kinds of support can be provided within the typical classroom routine?	Laptop computers, peer tutoring, aide in classroom, collaborative teaching
Time	Can the amount of time allotted for the lesson or for meeting the objective be adjusted?	Extended time, flexible due dates, testing accommodations
Degree of participation	Can the student participate in the lesson even though s/he cannot meet the objective? Is the participation meaningful to outcomes for that student?	Social interaction, language development, participation in cooperative groups
Alternative goals	Can alternative outcomes for an individual student be met by using the activity planned for the class?	Cooperative learning, peer tutoring, language development, students with significant disabilities
Substitute curriculum	Can the student work on a different activity that meets an appropriate outcome while the class is participating in the lesson?	Use of instructional aides, students with significant disabilities

7. Evaluate the effectiveness of adaptations; monitor and adjust while teaching. (Ebeling et al., 1994, p. 15)

Interventions in Individual Classrooms:
Validated Inclusive Practices

Fisher, Schumaker, and Deshler (1996) have examined the literature on inclusive practice to determine which practices have been empirically validated. They were also concerned about the level to which practices intrude on the curriculum and how practical they are for teachers to implement. They conducted a literature review in which they looked for studies of inclusive practices that had occurred in general education classrooms in which students with mild disabilities were included and the academic performance of these students was reported. Their review yielded six categories of inclusive practices, which, in turn, were analyzed for their effect on academic performance of all students in the classroom and their practicality for classroom teachers.

Peer Tutoring

Peer tutoring is a widely used intervention in which a student (the tutor) provides instruction for another (the tutee). Effective peer tutoring requires that tutors be trained in the processes of tutoring, teachers closely supervise tutoring sessions, the progress of tutees be systematically monitored, and tutoring occur regularly (Jenkins & Jenkins, 1985). Fisher et al. (1996) have identified two models of peer tutoring that meet the criteria for their study of inclusive practices.

Classwide peer tutoring (Delquadri, Greenwood, Stretton, & Hall, 1983; Delquadri, Greenwood, Whorton, Carta, & Hall, 1986; Greenwood, Delquadri, & Hall, 1984) is a peer-tutoring regimen in which "a class is divided into two teams that engage in competitions for a 1- to 2-week period" (Fisher et al., 1996, p. 125). Working in pairs, students follow a teacher-prepared peer-tutoring plan. Teams accumulate points when tutoring pairs provide correct answers during tutoring sessions. At the end of the 1- or 2-week period, the class is given a test, and class members' scores are totaled for their teams. The team with the highest number of tutoring points and test points wins the competition. Classwide peer tutoring has been studied to determine its effects on spelling achievement (Delquadri, Greenwood, Stretton, & Hall, 1983), acquisition of facts in social studies and science (Pomerantz, Windell, & Smith, 1994), and "tenth grade students recall of social studies content" (Fisher et al., 1996, p. 126). Phillips, Hamlet, Fuchs, and Fuchs (1993) have combined classwide peer touring with curriculum-based measurement. In this model, students "work in pairs on skills matched to their individual abilities. The hope was that through this differentiated instruction, student achievement on basic skills would improve" (Fisher et al., 1996, p. 127).

Studies of classwide peer tutoring have indicated that students with mild disabilities achieve more effectively when this strategy is used, and students and teachers were enthusiastic about the intervention. However, these studies examined the acquisition of factual information. Whether classwide peer tutoring would have similar effects on the acquisition of more complex knowledge and skills remains questionable. In addition, the practical effect on classroom time of classwide peer-tutoring models has not been systematically examined.

Cooperative Learning

Cooperative learning is a model of practice in which students are organized into four or five member teams for the purpose of accomplishing instructional tasks. Fisher, Schumaker, and Deshler (1996) identified three models of cooperative learning that were effective in increasing the academic achievement of students with disabilities in inclusive classrooms.

Slaven, Madden, and Leavey (1984a, 1984b) have developed team- assisted individualization, in which teams of four or five students support one another as each works on individualized tasks. They have studied team-assisted individualization's effects on math instruction with mixed results. In one study (1984a), they found no significant difference in achievement when students who participated in team-assisted individualization were compared with a group of students who participated in traditional math instruction over a 12-week period. In another study (1984b) that occurred over a 24-week period, all students, including those with disabilities, scored significantly higher than their traditionally instructed peers.

Cooperative integrated reading and composition (CIRC) is used to provide basal reading, reading comprehension, and integrated language arts instruction in the elementary grades (Slaven, Stevens, & Madden, 1988). Students work in cooperative teams, and they are asked to read with their parents each night. Their study indicated that students with disabilities scored significantly higher in reading and writing after a 24-week intervention. In a later study, Jenkins, Jewell, Leicester, Jenkins, and Troutner (1991) combined CIRC with a schoolwide inclusive practice model, but their analysis found no significant academic effect for students with or without disabilities.

Maheady, Sacca, and Harper (1988) have reported on their use of classwide student tutoring teams in which teams of students use a teacher-prepared lesson to acquire math skills and content. Students participate in an iterative problem-solving process, the goal of which is to support one another until each team member has solved a given math problem correctly. Maheady et al.'s (1988) study indicates that this method improved students' acquisition of 9th- and 10th-grade math skills for students' with disabilities and that their quiz scores also improved.

Fisher et al. (1996) suggest that these cooperative learning interventions might be important strategies for use in inclusive practice, provided that sufficient time is available for the interventions to work and that they are implemented according to the developers' specifications. However, Fisher et al. (1996) also indicate some reservations about their practicality, since small class size, time, teacher satisfaction, and the addition of new curricula are all required for the interventions to be implemented as developed.

Teaching Devices

Fisher et al. (1996) describe *teaching devices* as mechanisms teachers use "to mediate student understanding, storage, recall, and/or application of content" (p. 132). Of the variety of teaching devices described in instructional literature, graphic organizers and study guides met the criteria for their study.

Graphic organizers "are visual displays teachers use to organize information in a manner that makes the information easier to understand and learn" (Fisher et al., 1996, p. 132). Horton, Lovitt, and Bergerud have conducted three studies of their use and found that teacher- and student-directed graphic organizers proved to be useful tools for improving student performance. According to Horton,

Lovitt, and Bergerud (1990), graphic organizers help students see the information to be learned as a whole rather than as unconnected bits of information.

When they use study guides, teachers sort through often poorly written and difficult-to-understand text to focus students on important content. Horton and Lovitt (1989) have studied the effects of teacher-directed study guides in middle- and high school social studies and science classes. In their study, all students, including those with disabilities, were significantly more successful at grasping main ideas. Horton and Lovitt (1989) have also reported on the effects of student-directed study guides with similar results. Horton, Lovitt, Givens, and Nelson (1989) have studied the effects of study guides that are delivered via computer, and their results indicate that all students performed significantly better; students reported that they preferred the computer-delivered study guide to their textbooks. Higgins and Boone (1992) have also reported on computer-driven study guides, and although their results were not statistically significant, they indicate that the use of this approach was favorable.

In their analysis, Fisher et al. (1996) indicate that teaching devices are useful in improving academic performance, that failing students who use them are more likely to improve to passing, that the curriculum remains intact, and that teaching devices have been shown to be useful at a variety of levels, with a variety of content, and in a variety of teaching situations. These authors have reservations about the amount of time required for teachers to prepare graphic organizers and study guides, and the degree to which teachers were satisfied with their use.

Content Enhancement Routines

Content enhancement routines "help teachers carefully organize and deliver content information and help students identify, organize, comprehend, and recall critical content information" (Fisher et al., 1996, p. 136). Organizational routines, understanding routines, and a recall routine have been identified as particularly useful in inclusive practice.

Organizational routines "create frameworks for understanding the structure of presented content" (Fisher et al., 1996, p. 137). Prior to teaching a lesson, teachers orient students to the topic under consideration, ascertain their interest and prior knowledge, use teaching devices to present content, and define terms. Lenz, Alley, and

Schumaker (1987) have used this process to develop a *lesson organizer routine*, and Lenz, Marrs, Schumaker, and Deshler (1993) have developed a unit organizer routine. Results from studies of both these routines indicate that students' performance improved substantially and that teachers planned to continue using them.

Using *understanding routines*, teachers link the new concepts to be taught to knowledge students already have. Fisher et al. (1996) state that understanding routines "help students comprehend and acquire new information by specifying what concept is going to be learned, accessing the knowledge students possess relative to the new concept, explicitly depicting information related to the new concept in a graphic organizer, connecting student knowledge to the new concept, and summarizing what has been learned in a brief written statement" (p. 138). The *concept mastery routine* (Bulgren, Deshler, & Schumaker, 1993), *concept anchoring routine* (Bulgren, Schumaker, & Deshler, 1994) and *concept comparison routine* (Bulgren, Lenz, Schumaker, & Deshler, 1995) have all been shown to yield significantly better performance with all students, including those with disabilities. Teachers report that they continue to use the routines, thus testifying to their practicality, and students report their satisfaction with this approach to teaching. Deshler and Schumaker (1988) report on their use of a *recall routine*, in which teachers use mnemonic devices to facilitate recall of information. Their study indicates that the recall routine yields significant improvements in performance.

Understanding routines have been shown to be useful in improving student achievement, and they appear to be popular with teachers and students. However, Fisher et al. (1996) are cautious about their use, since students with disabilities did not always move into the passing range on tests, even though they improved significantly. They are concerned that students must be taught to use the routines, which may result in their not being used by teachers who do not have the time to provide this additional instruction. In addition, creating content enhancement routines takes considerable time, which teachers may not be able to give.

Curriculum Revision

Curriculum revision has been receiving some attention as a method of improving students' acquisition of content. The BIG Accommodations Program, a product of the University of Oregon Center to

Improve the Tools of Educators, is designed to improve students' higher-order thinking (Fisher et al., 1996). This project uses interactive videodiscs to teach students important concepts that underlie disciplinary content. Although results are preliminary, they have been encouraging. Students have shown significant gains in content acquisition and are motivated to use the materials.

Strategies Instruction

Strategies instruction is concerned with teaching students how to learn to use the knowledge they have acquired. Three learning strategies have been shown to be effective as inclusive practices: *model-lead-test* strategy instruction, the *strategies intervention* model, and the *strategies integration* approach.

In the model-lead-test strategy, the teacher first models the use of a learning strategy for students and then provides opportunities for practice. The students are then tested on their use of the strategy, and when they are able to score 80% or better on two successive tests, they are no longer instructed on the use of the strategy. The goal is to teach students to use strategies independently (Idol, 1987).

In the strategies intervention model, students first learn to use learning strategies, then adapt and apply them to their educational settings (Deshler & Schumaker, 1988). Learning strategies have been used quite successfully with students with mild disabilities in resource rooms, particularly as efforts to prepare the students for regular classroom instruction. Regular classroom teachers have recognized the usefulness of learning strategies instruction for many students who are disorganized learners or who lack the academic readiness to perform to high standards.

The strategies integration approach uses classroom content to teach students learning strategies. Students are introduced to a particular strategy; teachers model its use with classroom content; and students are given practice opportunities with the strategy using classroom content (Scanlon, Deshler, & Schumaker, 1996; Scanlon, Schumaker, & Deshler, 1994).

Learning strategies have been shown to be successful instructional interventions for all students, particularly those with mild disabilities. However, they require considerable teacher and classroom time.

Interventions by Sets of Teachers

A Process for Collaborative Problem Solving

In our professional development interactions with teachers at all grade levels, we have used a set of process steps for collaborative problem solving, developed by Pugach and Johnson (1990). These steps provide a systematic approach to collaboration, which teachers like as they enter this unfamiliar territory. Teachers generate ideas to solve real classroom problems, and they learn to work together and to see the value of a collaborative approach to practice. Their major concern is how to arrange the time necessary to work together when the current schedule and structure of their schools keeps them apart. Collaborative planning time is essential if we expect teachers to use collaboration skills in solving educational problems.

In training teachers to use collaborative problem solving, we use the process described in Table 8.3. We ask that one teacher present a problem involving a student or a curricular or instructional issue to a group of three or four colleagues to develop a clear understanding of the nature of the problem and to generate solutions and a plan of action. We emphasize that it is necessary to follow a structured process to allow teachers to learn working together systematically. It is important to note that teachers often claim to use these processes informally. However, it is the systematic use of collaborative problem solving that will yield the most results in schools.

Collaborative Instruction

Perhaps no innovation changes schools more fundamentally than *collaborative teaching*. Schools have traditionally been places where work was divided in ways that separated employees from one another, and teachers worked alone (Lortie, 1975). Teachers are prepared for solitary work, and evaluation systems focus on individual behavior. Curriculum is divided into discrete subjects that are not intended to overlap, and instruction is organized into sequences and specialties that stand alone to address the needs of categories of students. Even assessment results are organized and reported so that the individual teacher can be held accountable for student success or failure. In traditionally organized schools, it is assumed that teach-

TABLE 8.3
Collaborative Problem Solving

Process Steps (Pugach & Johnson, 1990)	*Questions to Ask*
1. Articulation of the problem	1. In clear, practical terms, what is the problem?
2. Consideration of contributing factors	2. What classroom and individual ingredients maintain the problem?
3. Development of a problem pattern statement	3. When and how often does the problem occur? How do the students, their classmates, and the teacher respond? What elements of the problem and classroom environment can be controlled?
4. Generation of possible solutions	4. What are at least three plausible remedies to the problem?
5. Selection of the solution	5. Which solution does the teacher prefer? What does the teacher predict will occur when the solution is implemented?
6. Development of an evaluation plan	6. How will the teacher know whether the solution works?
7. Implementation and monitoring of the identified solution	7. When will the solution be implemented? How long will the teacher continue to use the solution? How will the team follow up on progress toward the solution?

ing and learning can be organized bureaucratically and that divisions of labor can be created that manages any dysfunction that might arise as students are processed through the system.

The schools we envision reject the assumption that schools are professional bureaucracies that can create subsystems to process student failure. The social and economic demands of the 21st century will not allow schools to continue their practice of using methods of sorting and selecting (Spring, 1989) to determine which students are deserving of educational excellence. Society and the economy now demand that everyone be a responsible citizen, a productive worker, and a committed contributor to community life, and that education is the institution responsible for providing young people with the knowledge, skills, and dispositions necessary to be responsible, productive, and committed. Responding to these challenges requires that schools use all the talents and resources available to them and that they use their resources in ways that maximize results. The private sector has shown that collaborative work teams can work to accomplish improved productivity in a variety of settings. It is our view that schools must adapt this important approach in order to meet the challenges that face them.

Collaboration in schools involves two distinct but related initiatives, one in curriculum and one in instruction. Although each can be undertaken separately, combining them can yield benefits that each individually will not. In curriculum, collaboration entails bringing together the distinct subjects of the curriculum as it is now compartmentalized into an interdisciplinary body of knowledge, skills, and dispositions that are important for all learners. In instruction, collaboration entails teachers' working together to pool their knowledge, skills, dispositions, and approaches to deliver the curriculum successfully to all learners. Our understanding of collaboration recognizes that teachers have traditionally been trained as subject-area or developmental specialists who learn on the job about the demands of teaching students having diverse needs.

Cook and Friend (1995) argue that co-teaching as a model of collaboration can be defined as "two or more professionals delivering substantive instruction to a diverse, or blended, group of students in a single physical space" (p. 93). We can see from this definition that Cook and Friend consider co-teaching to be a professional activity that addresses the needs of the diverse learners in a classroom. The authors suggest that co-teaching increases the availability of alternatives in instruction for all students, that instruction can be delivered more intensively, that students with special needs are not singled out when they require additional help, and that teachers are more able to support one another when they co-teach.

Teachers have been encouraged to experiment with collaboration in an effort to provide the support students with disabilities need when they are included in general education classrooms. However, there are several issues that teachers who are interested in collaboration should consider before they take the plunge into this new work arrangement:

1. Teachers are sometimes territorial about their skills and their ability to control the classroom. Before they co-teach, teachers should discuss the degree to which they are willing to give up their autonomy, control, and physical space. Working with another individual in a collaborative relationship requires that each party be willing to share expertise, authority, and personal space.

2. Teachers who collaborate not only see one another's skills and strengths; they also see one another's weaknesses. Before they enter into a collaborative relationship, each teacher should think about how it would feel to have another person present for a bad day or a lesson that extends beyond the teacher's skills. Recognizing that one cannot know and do everything in the classroom is an important prerequisite to collaboration.

3. To some degree, teachers believe that they possess the single best way to teach, whether that sense applies to a set of lessons or one's general approach. Obviously, the presence in a classroom of two people who each believe that s/he is the sole owner of the best way to teach is a situation ripe for conflict. Before beginning collaborative teaching, teachers should discuss their approaches to teaching, those approaches that work best for them, and how they can accommodate one another's pedagogical peccadilloes.

4. Professional educators who work together will disagree with one another about crucial items like students, curriculum, approaches, and assessments and about relatively trivial issues like use of a desk, how to begin class, and what color ink to use when grading. Professionals who collaborate successfully have to figure out ways to mediate their disputes and concerns so that they do not become a conflicted team over issues that are not substantive in the classroom. When issues arise that are substantive, collaborators must develop ways to disagree agreeably or to end their collaboration peaceably.

Working together as collaborators, whether it is called co-teaching as suggested by Friend and Bursuch (1996) or cooperative teaching as described by Hourcade and Bauwens (1996), requires the development of a professional relationship. Hourcade and Bauwens have identified five phases in this development:

1. Cooperative presence—two teachers share the same space but not necessarily the same tasks or responsibilities
2. Cooperative planning—two teachers plan for instruction together but deliver it separately
3. Cooperative presenting—teachers plan and present instruction together
4. Cooperative processing—two teachers plan and present instruction, then jointly try to understand what happened in order to make further plans
5. Cooperative problem solving—two teachers plan, present, and process instruction and use one another's knowledge and skills to develop new approaches to instruction that are unique to their context

We can see from Hourcade and Bauwens's (1996) analysis that collaborating teachers who have reached the cooperative problem-solving phase are working together in new ways to provide instruction in the classroom. As their relationship develops, they are able to define tasks and responsibilities jointly and to make decisions as though they were one. Becoming this proficient at collaboration requires a commitment to working together and the time necessary for the relationship to develop.

Integrated Learning

Educators have traditionally thought about their practice in compartmentalized terms. Although this approach may have been helpful in bureaucratically organized schools and practices, educators who are working to transform their schools into democratic organizations that are responsive to individual needs recognize that they will need an integrated approach that encourages them to think about their practices holistically. We offer the framework graphically depicted in Figure 8.1 to assist educators in their efforts to conceptualize integrated learning.

Figure 8.1. Integrated Learning

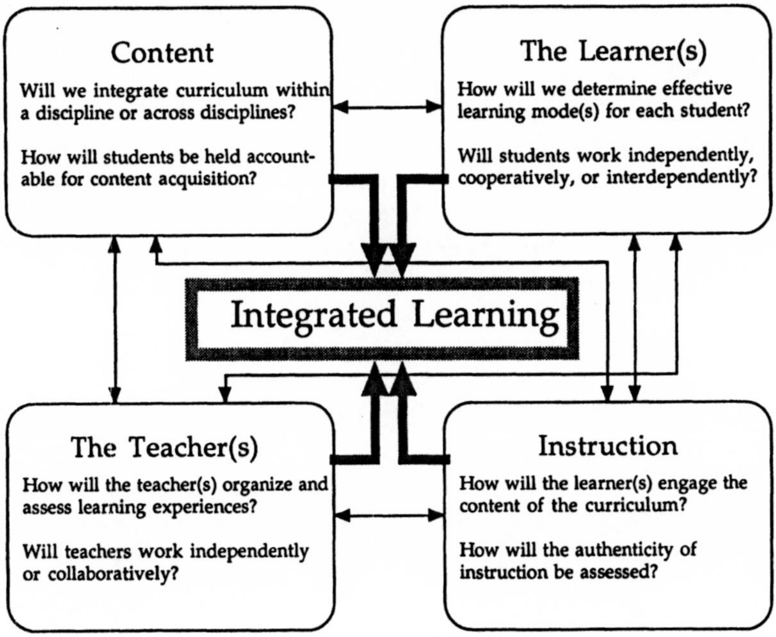

Content

As educators consider the content of the curriculum, they must begin to think across disciplinary boundaries to envision learning that is integrated rather than compartmentalized. Making efforts to attach significance to the content to be learned by creating connections to the life experiences of students will encourage teachers to draw upon knowledge that crosses the lines that have been drawn in the curriculum by subject-area specialists. In addition, focusing on higher-order thinking, critical thinking, and problem solving enables the creation of course content and assignments that stimulate students to use their minds creatively and flexibly and to use knowledge in ways that are meaningful to them.

Students should also be held accountable for the acquisition of content in ways that are meaningful and integrated. Assessments should be constructed to require students to understand and apply knowledge in ways that force them to construct new knowledge, thereby joining instruction and assessment. A variety of assessment tools should be used to evaluate the student's acquisition of content, including paper-and-pencil tests, projects, performances, problem solving, and service learning. Integrating content and the tools used to assess its acquisition provides teachers, students, and the public with a more detailed description of what students must learn and the degree to which they have accomplished those learning standards set forth for them. When curriculum becomes integrated, teachers and administrators must spend more time educating the public about curricular content and providing a public understanding of the purposes of the curriculum.

Learners

Educators have long recognized that individual students learn in individual ways. With the advent of learning-styles theory and theories of multiple intelligences, researchers have urged educators to use new understandings of the way learners conceptualize content and create meaning from it. Educators have not been so quick to implement these understandings, in part because accountability schemes continue to emphasize logico-mathematical learning and recall. In addition, although many educators can profess a familiarity with the theories of learning styles and multiple intelligences, they have neither been trained in, nor held accountable for, their integration into classroom practices and routines. As a result, much instruction continues to consist of telling large groups of students what to do, asking them whether they understand, and telling them what they have been told. Perhaps no educational reform could have a greater long-term effect than requiring teachers to plan for small group instruction and that they produce at least two instructional approaches for every lesson.

Individualizing instruction to address differences in learning approaches provides the opportunity to differentiate instruction by varying how students perform instructional tasks. Some tasks, and some students, are most successful when they are addressed independently. And certainly, learning to think for oneself, organizing one's own approach, and becoming an independent learner and worker are important skills for all students. However, students must also learn to work together, and cooperative learning has become quite popular and successful as a tool for developing a collaborative work ethic and improving performance among students.

Stephen Covey (1989), in his book, *The Seven Habits of Highly Successful People*, suggests that interdependence is the highest form of human relationship. When people work interdependently, they realize the power of the connections between them and create new meanings from their work. In cooperative work, according to Covey, people influence group effort by adding their own unique contribution to the task, but they do not necessarily take changed perspectives or new learning away from the task. Tasks done cooperatively could be accomplished, although not necessarily as productively, without the assistance of each group member. Interdependent work requires that all workers contribute in order to accomplish the task, and as a result, all workers are vital and carry away new understandings.

Organizing instructional tasks that are intended to be accomplished interdependently may be the goal of many cooperative learning activities, but a common criticism of cooperative learning is that some students (usually those most able) dominate the assignment and as a result the group gets the credit for a few students' work. Structuring activities for interdependence for a group of diverse learners is indeed a challenge. However, the learning productivity that results is worth the thought and energy necessary.

Teachers

Organizing integrated learning is a challenge for teachers because it affects two foundations of educational practices—the disciplinary organization of knowledge and the solitary work of teachers. Although many teachers could organize an integrated instructional unit, combining integrated curriculum, instruction, and assessment across the duration of a school year would tax the time and energy of most teachers, because this approach requires a more comprehensive understanding of the purposes of learning than we have expected teachers to have. Integrated learning also requires that teachers have knowledge across disciplines and that they understand how to use a variety of assessment approaches to ascertain whether students have acquired the desired knowledge and can use it effectively. Because teachers have not been trained to do these tasks and are not expected to do them—even on a limited basis—by existing curriculum and assessment structures, they are poorly prepared to address integrated learning. That is not to say that the ability to create integrated approaches is sorely lacking in a school. We are saying that individual teachers are not capable of integrating learning, not because of their lack of capability, but because it is unreasonable to expect a teacher working alone to have sufficient knowledge, skills, time, and energy to integrate learning comprehensively.

If teachers are to be expected to integrate learning experiences for all students, new arrangements that support teachers' working collaboratively must be created, and collaborative work must replace solitary teaching as the norm in schools. Covey's conceptualizations of cooperation and interdependence are both helpful in conceptualizing new work relationships for teachers. Some instructional tasks can be approached cooperatively so that each partner in the task at hand takes a part of the work to be done, completes it independently, then fits it into the cooperative response that it being prepared by the instructional team. Certainly, some specialization and division of labor can reduce the stress of creating instructional plans that address the needs of all students. However, certain levels of interdependence must also be fostered if the instructional team is to become a learning organization (Senge, 1990) that can respond to the needs of all learners as instruction proceeds.

Our comments about the challenges of interdependent learning also apply to collaborative teaching arrangements in which teachers are expected to work interdependently, and they are probably compounded by teachers' independent work habits. To implement interdependent work relationships, teachers will have to become aware of the variety of knowledge traditions and skills that make up educational practices, understand their implications for meeting the needs of all students, implement a variety of teaching techniques and create new ones that synthesize knowledge traditions, and most important, think about their practices holistically.

Instruction

The diversity in learning characteristics of the students who occupied our classrooms at the turn of the century has been well documented, but it never ceases to mystify practitioners. When we take teachers through grouping exercises, they quickly come to understand that no two students are alike and that groups are artificial organizing structures. They come to recognize that the only viable group, if we use student characteristics to set parameters, is a group of one. However, practitioners also recognize that managing learning for 25 groups of one is untenable. They understand the need to create new instructional strategies that meet all students' needs, but they are neither prepared to do so nor expected to do so by existing institutional arrangements.

Creating new instructional approaches requires that teachers work collaboratively to combine teaching strategies such as cooperative learning, peer tutoring, small group instruction, independent learning, and use of electronic media to plan, implement, and manage lessons in the classroom. Integrating learning means that the images like the sage on the stage or the shepherd and his flock are no longer applicable to the classroom. The teacher becomes a facilitator of learning—a guide, a coach—who sets the instructional course and teaches students to steer their own learning course toward established learning destinations. The teacher oversees the learning environment, provides students access to information, and assesses student progress, not like the English headmaster but more like a guardian angel who protects the students' interests and urges them toward the good. We might also add that we are not advocating adult abdication of the expert role, such as often was the case in the open school movement when students made their own curricular and instructional decisions. We are suggesting that students learn to take a role in instructional decision making and that they be held accountable for their decisions. To accomplish this, teachers must maintain a gentle but firm hand on the instructional rudder and use the throttle judiciously to correct for student missteps, errors in judgment, and lack of attention to the course of learning.

The Teacher as Director

The director in the playhouse metaphor is constantly seeking the interpretation that the actors bring to the play and its production. The actors are asked not only to portray the character but to *be* the character: to be the character who can love and hate, who is energized and despondent, who speaks but also listens actively and attentively to others. The part may require more than fluctuating emotional states; it may require physical action or refined movement, the ability to dance, sing, or play an instrument. The issue in the play or in the classroom is the actor as instrument and the director as facilitator. The actor as performer or student as inquirer is an instrument, someone who creates a performance or produces an outcome. In both cases, it is the individual performance that counts, along with their interpretation of its meaning and relevance to their particular context. The teacher as director or teacher as choreographer must start with the individual student and seek their interpretation of the part or the standard to be learned. Until the individual students can grasp the meaning for themselves, they cannot proceed with enthusiasm and purpose.

The director uses many of the same modeling and teaching techniques that teachers use to assist the actor to give his best performance. Imitation, modeling, visualization, repetition, and practicing the routine are common for both types of facilitators. The director uses the company as the teacher uses the peer group to provide support for individual learning. The pressure to sort individual students from first to last on each required performance hinders the ability of teachers to use the peer group to create the same unifying theme that binds members of the class like members of the company.

Finally, the playhouse recognizes all the participants in the production from director to stagehand. Much of the work of the production is integrated and collaborative. We have been expecting teachers to teach a diverse student population alone. Historically, there has been some discussion of differentiated roles in schools. For the most part, the culture of schools negates any role that does not resemble the teaching role. General or regular teachers refuse to accept anyone who does not do what they do as a peer. The need to examine the conditions of teaching, and the means of supporting teachers in classrooms requires breaking the boundary of what we call a classroom. The isolation of teachers is the most significant barrier to building a learning community that grows in its capacity to meet the challenges of more complex productions.

9

Thinking Differently About Evaluation

Moving Beyond the Paradox

Why do our special education programs cost so much? Do we really need the Cadillac?

Why do we have so many students in special education? Do they all really need to be there?

We're in compliance, but does that mean we have quality programs?

Are our programs as good as we think they are? How can we get better?

Is our service delivery model the right one for our district? Are there others we should be considering? What other models are there, and what data are there to support the various models of practice?

We've recently had a change in leadership. Our director of student support retired after serving in the position for 22 years. We'd like an evaluation to help us think about our future direction.

We believe that inclusion has helped our students with disabilities. We want to know if inclusion is having a negative influence on our highest-achieving students.

We have a large number of instructional assistants (aides, teacher or personal assistants, paraprofessionals). Do we really need to have so many?

How have we responded to these questions? What data can be brought to bear on such an inquiry? How have we gone about collecting, analyzing, interpreting, and reporting these data? How were the evaluations received, used, and incorporated; how did they transform the work of school staff? What have we learned from our evaluation research as we have responded to these and similar questions? What recommendations do we have for practitioners with regard to evaluating their own programs?

Throughout this book, we have shared much from what we have learned through our visits to, and evaluation studies at, various school districts across the country. In this chapter, we explore the process and the nature of program evaluation as we see it and some of what we have learned from engaging in this inquiry and reflection. We explore some of these aspects of evaluating educational programs in general and outline our application notes with regard to evaluating programs that serve all students, including those with disabilities. Finally, we offer a framework that we have developed through our work for districts' self-study. We learned a great deal as we conducted these studies and hope that, as we pass these lessons on, practitioners will understand the value of reflection and evaluation.

As we think about changing whole systems, we know that evaluation is a powerful lever for moving districts toward unified systems and schools toward learner-centeredness. Given the concepts of physics and motion we have used metaphorically throughout this book, the question becomes, Where do we place the fulcrum to create leverage points for change? Each of the questions posed initially in this chapter can be addressed more fully by reflecting on professional practice within the whole system—looking at the quality of the whole system, the numbers of students identified as having special needs, budget priorities and issues, change efforts, direction, and perhaps most important, the values of the system. After all, the root word in evaluation is *value*. In this particular setting, we ask practitioners to consider, What is valued for all students?

As we discuss more focused evaluation efforts, shining the light on specific areas of concern serves to illuminate particularly good work. Alternatively, evaluation may enlighten practitioners as to what needs to be done if the district is not implementing quality practice. Two major concepts emerge as we think about evaluating programs and services: the importance of continuous and reflective practice and the importance of making decisions that are based on sound data. The inquiry in which we engage needs to be purposeful and deliberate to be the most useful. As evaluators, our practice gauge was, What did we do, and how did we go about engaging in responsive evaluative inquiry?

The Value of Evaluation

Program evaluation is a distinct discipline that is intended to provide information about program functioning to decision makers. Scriven (1991) defines evaluation as "the process of determining the merit, worth and value of things" (p. vii). Patton (1997) describes program evaluation as

the systematic collection of information about the activities, characteristics, and outcomes of programs to make judgments about the program, improve program effectiveness, and/or informed decisions about future programming. Utilization-focused program evaluation (as opposed to program evaluation in general) is evaluation done for and with specific, intended primary users for specific, intended uses. (p. 23)

All program evaluations should be guided by the standards published by the Joint Committee on Standards for Educational Evaluation (1994). The joint committee, representing the major professional organizations from the United States and Canada, has been working to develop standards for educational evaluation for more than 25 years. These standards are the only educational standards approved by the American National Standards Institute (ANSI). In evaluating programs, personnel, and students, the standards address the four areas of utility, feasibility, propriety, and accuracy.

The joint committee has focused on a trilogy of evaluation foci for our purposes: personnel evaluation (1988), program evaluation (1994), and student evaluation (in press). The three types of evaluations do interface, but the considerations, politics, and technologies or strategies they employ are different. Evaluation is the description and judgment of the merit and worth of an evaluand and the entity being evaluated, the evaluation process drawing upon multiple assessments and data sources. Assessments are single measurements or tests or accounts of program, student, or personnel progress.

Sage and Burrello (1994) are specific about the potential uses that guide and focus evaluation in our field of work:

1. *Program improvement.* Evaluation serves as a management tool, helping the program administrator and his or her staff make specific suggestions in the planning and implementation of a program or service.
2. *Program review.* Evaluation serves as a means for top management to periodically review and audit the appropriateness of current program definition and scope and the quality of service delivery.
3. *Compliance monitoring.* Evaluation serves as a means for state agencies to assess whether program implementation is being conducted in accordance with state and federal laws and regulations.
4. *Securing political and fiscal support.* Evaluation serves as a means to secure, maintain, and increase school patronage and taxpayer support for increased school funding and participation in school activities.
5. *Policy analysis.* Evaluation as policy analysis is an activity initiated by policymakers to help them decide whether to change, terminate, or reauthorize existing policies governing a program or practice.
6. *Provision of information to the community.* Evaluation is conducted to provide information about the characteristics of an education program to the community. It recognizes value pluralism and seeks to represent a range of interests in issue formulation. The basic goal is an informed citizenry, and the evaluator acts as broker in exchanges of information between different groups.

We are only as good as our questions. Asking good questions and planning to respond to them well is a critical part of evaluation design. Only when the questions and uses of future information are clear can the process or methodology be designed. When embarking on an evaluation, one needs to push for extreme clarity, honesty, and intentionality. When we begin a program evaluation, we translate the academic discourse on evaluation into practitioners' language by asking questions such as

- What are your hunches with regard to the answers to your questions?
- What kinds of data do you collect now?
- How thoughtful have you been about your own practice?
- Have you conducted any self-study?
- What have you learned upon such reflection?
- If you have not conducted any such inquiry, have you reflected on why not?
- What guesses or hunches do you have about the questions you have about your program?
- What data would be compelling enough for you to have your questions addressed adequately?
- How will you use the new information?
- Who will use the new information?
- Will your use of such data make a difference for students?
- Can you live with the results?

The disciplines of program evaluation have come to value reflective practice, continual self-study, and the necessity of being informed about various frameworks for evaluating and reflecting on good practice. Unfortunately, many practitioners cite time and expertise as good reasons for their avoidance of things evaluative. In conducting our various evaluation studies, we have noticed that questions and concerns about programs are often symptoms that signal far deeper, more fundamental problems within the system. We have come to recognize the importance of identifying contextual and political factors in the whole system, including special education. Vigilance in leadership helps to shape the need for evaluation and it requires building a consensus about purpose and use.

Purposes, intended uses, and questions should drive good evaluations and should determine such things as whether or not to proceed with an evaluation if in fact it is an evaluation that is needed to inform on the work at hand. Whether or not to proceed, who (internal or external, individual or team) will be best suited for the work at hand, who will have the necessary credibility to produce the findings or report, who wants to know and what they want to know are all critical design elements to address prior to beginning the study.

Paradoxes in Program Evaluation

Managing the paradox, a theme throughout our book, involves managing paradoxes about evaluation as well. We introduce seven paradoxes about the findings from our studies and about the processes of our inquiry in order to help practitioners think about program evaluation.

Paradox 1:
It Was the Best of Times, It Was the Worst of Times

As a culture, we have a love-hate relationship with evaluation. Evaluation can help solve problems; evaluation can uncover or cause problems. We prefer receiving a clean bill of health from our internist and our automobile mechanic, and we clean our houses for our cleaners. When we hear the regulatory or compliance monitoring staff call to say that help is on its way, we are neither amused nor poised for assistance.

When districts request or embark on a study, there is usually a commitment to improve, to change, to share responsibility, to collaborate, to look for a new way of working. Often, individuals or groups are entrenched in their modes of operation and don't know how to move "out of the box," to practice differently. What used to work so well, or seemed to, no longer does. We have learned that most districts do not engage in self-study, do not have any formal process for reflection of practice or systematic review, and have not commissioned external studies. The process can be a dramatic and vulnerable experience internally, although the potential for positive influence and results is tremendous. Getting a district to the commitment stage for an evaluation inquiry is a deft and time-consuming task for district leadership. We commend the school districts that have ventured forth with such evaluation studies, conducted either internally or by external consultants.

Many districts across the nation struggle with challenging issues related to special education but do not take the initiative to undergo a study with the commitment to enact changes. This leaves the door open to surprise, suspicion, mistrust, and attack by outsiders, and for internal sabotage as well. Often, if there has been a changing of the guard at the top or a central office coup, there follow internal challenges to the status quo by both newcomers and existing power seekers, hoping to realign interests, practice, and resources within new agendas for the district.

Paradox 2:
Sailing Around in the Middle of the Ocean

Recreational sailors are known to say that they do not sail to get somewhere; when they sail, they are already where they want to be. Like these sailors, administrators and evaluators find themselves awash in their element, but unlike recreational sailors, they have destinations or benchmarks to reach. Administrators can gather cascades of data about their programs and still not know whether their programs are of value.

Administrators and evaluators can become overwhelmed and paralyzed by the notion of "doing it all." We used to talk in terms of how to conduct comprehensive evaluations, evaluating the complete program, with multiple stakeholder involvement, multiple methods, and so forth. We now believe that we may not live long enough to engage in such practice well, let alone make use of the reports and benefit from the results of such an ambitious enterprise. We know many a colleague who has begun such an ambitious task; the task is never brought to fruition and consequently is of no use to inform change. Does it make more sense to go very deep or very wide? It depends.

We have found that by going deep, we focus the study where there are particular questions, issues, and concerns, and simultaneously we open other venues to see the whole. Whereas we may enter an evaluation seeking to illuminate a particular set of questions, we enter like a light into a prism, illuminating our particular issues and concerns but also shining across the many other elements interacting within the structure and operations of the district or school organization as a whole. We believe that inquiry must begin with some focused questions, rather than through the comprehensive manner in which we used to operate. "We want to know how effective our programs are" is often euphemistic for some particular set of concerns. For example, questions about the high and rising costs of special education are often a statement about investing disproportionate amounts of money on students who have been historically devalued. We know that values and moral purpose are integral to making use of evaluation findings.

Paradox 3:
Special Education Program Evaluation Versus
Evaluation of the General Education Program

Given our earlier discussion of the two system archetypes suggested by Senge (1990), we believe special education is embedded in the common welfare that schools should pursue for all students. Since special education services essentially begin with a referral from a general educator's questions about a student's academic or social progress, special education is circumscribed by the educator's capacity to deal with differences. Evaluation of special services must necessarily include an assessment of the capacity of educators to serve all students in typical classrooms first.

The evaluation of programs that serve students with disabilities must be aligned with evaluation of all programs within general education and with professional development, organizational planning, and system change as well. Again, if program evaluation is the lever for change, where are the leverage points? Where should we place the fulcrum? We have found that the quality of a special education program usually reflects the quality of the general education program. We seldom see a spectacular general education program with poor special education services. And often, when special education needs significant shoring up, so does the entire educational offering. In more than one study, a strong cry for changes within the special education programs signaled symptoms of more fundamental needs for general education reform.

Special education personnel often work hard placing increasing numbers of marginal students into special education settings, thereby putting the fulcrum at the wrong leverage point. This enables regular education personnel to "do a better job" for the higher-achieving students. We hear concerns that special educators, particularly at the secondary level, command little respect from teachers of the various disciplines—math, science, foreign language—because they lack content expertise in the liberal arts, hard sciences, and so forth. We have heard for some time from special educators that their peers lack the pedagogical skills necessary to address the needs of all students: "They teach subjects, not students." In previous chapters, we have discussed such strategies as creating new teams of teachers, with both personnel who have exceptional content knowledge and others who have pedagogical knowledge and student behavioral expertise, for example. The process of developing a unified evaluation for general and special education creates opportunities for redeployment of scarce resources and marshals the knowledge, skills, and expertise that teachers have on behalf of all students, not simply those who are targeted for special treatment.

Special education is viewed as (in some contexts *is*) expanding and commanding more resources while the general education system loses its capacity to address the needs of diverse learners. If special education is the only ticket to receiving instructional assistance for any student, then well-meaning teachers and parents will refer increasing numbers of those students out of the classroom in order to access that system. As we have discussed at length, this does not help students. It may be perceived as helping classroom teachers, though we disagree that it does. Of course, as a result of this phenomenon, students continually move into the margins and are referred out until there is only one child remaining—a truly homogeneous classroom! The perceived or real lack of capacity of those within the general system to take responsibility and work with all students maintains an expensive, ineffective, and inefficient dual system.

Paradox 4:
Individualized Programs Versus
Standardized Education

Program evaluation is necessary in a student assessment-driven arena to understand why students are achieving to greater or lesser degrees than targeted. Why are our students achieving well or not achieving to high standards? Should we also look at program and personnel factors in addition to our focus on student assessments? We maintain that it is important here to be clear about purpose and use, particularly with regard to high-stakes student assessments.

What is really needed is individualized access to a standards-based curriculum. We have found that, in many cases, students with disabilities were not only not held to high standards, they were in fact held to no standards at all. Locally held standards are now the norm for judging student progress. Discovering the standards and their application used to be an anticipated outcome of our evaluation efforts. With the national movement to state standards and high-stakes testing for graduation, standards are now more clearly defined. Now the evaluation task becomes an effort to discover who uses the same standards and how accommodations and modifications are made for individual differences. To provide useful evaluative data, one must have a values orientation, clear moral purpose, and a sense of what is "good" education for all students, including those with disabilities.

Paradox 5:
Reflective Practitioners Versus
Biased Decision Makers

Evaluations can be conducted internally or by external consultants. If someone in a district has both the capacity and credibility to conduct the study, then an internal evaluation can be an effective and inexpensive strategy. Often, however, an external evaluator, consultant, or facilitator is necessary for the evaluation to command credibility and for the users to have confidence in its results. Evaluators can play a number of roles, including external expert, leader of a mixed group of insiders and outsiders, facilitator of an internal or community stakeholder group, a teacher for an internal leadership group, an auditor (or validator) of a self-study, or some combination of these. We recommend that any external evaluator use *Guiding Principles for Evaluators* from the American Evaluation Association (Shadish, Newman, Sheirer, & Wye, 1995), which addresses systematic inquiry, competence, honesty, integrity, respect for people, and responsibilities for general and public welfare.

Fetterman, Kaftarian, and Wandersman (1996) argue for an empowerment evaluation, in which groups get smart about their own investigative work and grow from it. We have learned that this is best done in evaluations that are intended to anticipate and solve problems or perhaps as an extension of some credible, more comprehensive evaluation effort. Empowerment evaluations do not work if there are already suspicions and mistrust among program stakeholders.

If an "insider" conducts an internal evaluation, a process must be in place to acknowledge and debrief his biases. Biases are not necessarily negative; they can also result in the evaluator's highlighting his favored positions. Or they may create a situation in which the evaluation becomes a platform for his own causes. The benefits and costs (attractors and detractors) of internal and external evaluations, and the possibility of combining them, rather than making an either-or decision, must be considered when a district prepares to assess its educational programs.

Paradox 6:
Perfectly Rigorous Evaluations Versus
Good-Enough Evaluations

The concept of attractors or incentives, which we used extensively in the five case studies presented in Chapter 4, apply to evaluations as well. Resolving a grievance, looking within a parent complaint or due process hearing, or responding to a new board member's agenda or a constituent's perception of an injustice are factors that surface the need for someone to conduct an evaluation. Policymakers who decide to commission an evaluation believe they are acting in a responsible way to right a wrong or to put things in perspective. Equity of services across schools is an often-urgent petition that policymakers hear from their constituents. Less frequently are they persuaded to reduce a discrepancy between demands for a more desirable alternative and current practice in the district and its schools. Most often we have learned that an attractor is reassurance and revalidation of the district's commitments and practices from an outsider because of the expense of the programs and the paucity of data available to justify many special education practices.

Complex adaptive systems (CAS) principles suggest that an evaluation inquiry is a formal way to listen to the shadow system of the district and tune in to its edges. The evaluation is an opportunity to invite and channel the criticism of the system's practices into an approved process that protects critics under the rules of confidentiality and anonymity. The shadow system uses informal relationships and perceptions of stakeholders to inform the leadership about how they see the mental models and actions of the system actors on their children and families. By tuning to the edge, the evaluation allows more diversity of opinion and fosters a different flow of information into the system, instead of reinforcing the way information is currently controlled and directed within the organization.

Complex adaptive science principles also suggest a framework for evaluation by using the district's "good-enough vision" to guide the evaluation. In their search for perfection, districts often try to compare their programs with flawless prototypes. Aligning the evaluation with a good-enough vision allows the district to examine what it does and develop strategies for improvement. Framing the evaluation through the way policymakers see the system and its potential to meet the expectations of the school-community for all students should guide the purpose and use of the evaluation.

Finally, CAS suggests that the outcome of the evaluation be judged in terms of how many different potential actions can be implemented. Although the evaluation should recommend multiple actions, it should not specify actions in detail. The process of implementation of recommendations should begin with a set of minimal specifications that suggest parameters for action and evaluation of those improvements. Implementation based on CAS principles should be the province of teams of professionals, parents, and others who need to be committed to resolving problems and have the expertise to consider novel ways of using the recommendations to improve both their practice and student learning.

Paradox 7:
Formative Versus Summative Evaluations

We have portrayed three major discourses in the recent history of special education and how our collective work has progressed and focused. We have seen a heightened interest in accountability, as well as a fairly common set of questions that reflect some fundamental issues in the progression of special education programs. We have also seen evaluation of special education programs change and shift through the three discourses. Evaluation of special education programs has focused on a variety of outcomes and purposes: compliance monitoring, assessment of consumer satisfaction or student well-being, access to general education, access to results, access to achieving the same high standards expected of all students. Our work suggests that important nuances and transformations in both programs and evaluation approaches have occurred.

Continuum of Services. Within this discourse, we saw a preoccupation with compliance with the law, access to an education, structural and human resources inputs, and the provision of a wide array of possible placements and services. This stage was very much grounded in the law and regulations, and it was conducted by special education professionals primarily—often in the form of state or federal government agents. Judgments were made by specialists, not by participatory groups, although consumers, parents, and advocates had input. The evaluation of quality took a back seat to compliance monitoring; in this perspective "a compliant program is a quality program."

Inclusion. When the inclusive schools discourse was in place, attention was focused on achieving access to the general education classroom for students with disabilities. Unfortunately, this sometimes came at the expense of assessment of achievement of high standards and appropriate student learning. The emphasis shifted to the quality of programs—primarily structural and human resources inputs—but not necessarily at quality of learner achievement and results of education. Evaluation also became more formative and inclusive of participants and other stakeholders, particularly parents and some of our older, secondary students.

Unified System. The unified systems discourse has occurred in a policy environment in which the focus on inputs has shifted to an emphasis on the measurement of outcomes and more attention is given to results than to the process by which they are achieved. Program evaluation, as it has been represented in accountability policy, asks three questions: (a) Are all students being held accountable? (b) How are all students doing? (c) Are all students learning to very high standards? Under the provisions of IDEA 97, school districts are held accountable for students' with disabilities access to the regular education curriculum, the quality of programs, and the degree to which students with disabilities achieve very high standards. Achievement of very high standards has become the mantra for all students.

In a unified system, evaluation begins with describing and judging the quality and results of regular education, and then the education of students with disabilities within the larger context. Assessing the strengths of general education, the needs of the larger system, and how those needs affect special education causes the strengths and weaknesses of the provision of programs and services to students with disabilities to be judged. No longer are the issues ones of access and program inputs or compliance-type indicators for programs. The questions we ask in evaluations of unified systems are (a) Are students with disabilities held to the same very high standards as their nonhandicapped peers? (b) Are students with disabilities held to any standards? (c) Are all students included in high- stakes testing? (d) When the data from state- or district-wide assessments and IEPs are considered, how are students doing?

Reflections on Our Evaluation Practice

Our work with school districts has given us many opportunities to observe and evaluate change processes in special education. As we have reflected upon our work, several areas of consideration (see Table 9.1 and Resource B) have emerged from our efforts to look at the system under study within the framework of the unified system. These are the questions we have focused on the following:

- What are the strengths of the whole system?
- What are the soft spots?
- What is the vision?
- Given the strengths and weaknesses of the whole system, what are the implications, challenges, and opportunities for educating students with disabilities and other special needs?
- How does professional practice, in general, influence how students with special needs are educated?

We offer the following notes and methodological guidance to assist districts as they prepare to evaluate their educational programs. Following are some examples of our reflections.

Purposes, Visions, and Hallucinations

Many districts lack an overarching statement of moral purpose, whether they call it a vision, mission, or statement of values, and

TABLE 9.1
Program Evaluation Self-Study Components

Desired Practice Components	*Subcomponents*
Vision, governance, and policy	Shared mind-set Governance/policy Specific policy issues Leadership and management Intellectual capital and competence
Developing and improving the educational program for all students	Core programming Preschool programming Transitional programming Technology
Developing and maintaining the educational climate and learning	Environment
Developing and involving the community of stakeholders	
Developing and monitoring fiscal resources	
Performance orientation and consequences	Performance orientation Consequences
Capacity for change	

many of these statements exist on paper only. They are not in the hearts of stakeholders, nor are they embedded in the district's practices. They are often loftily stated hallucinations about a better world of schools—well-intentioned, generating warm, fuzzy feelings, even fun to think about, but of little practical value and rarely ennobling or empowering. Schools and school districts need a grounded statement of purposes that define stakeholders' valued future so that policy development, program planning, and school operations are tied together. We cannot emphasize enough the importance of a commonly shared, good-enough vision that acts as an attractor for program improvement.

Instructional Capacity and Competence

The least-qualified personnel often deliver instruction to the most instructionally needy or vulnerable students. There is, in many schools, an overreliance on paraprofessionals, and the current shortage of teachers often means that teachers who are knowledgeable about or skilled in the knowledge tradition in special education are assigned to work with the students most difficult to teach. In addition, special educators spend a considerable amount of their time on bureaucratic tasks that detract from instruction. Just as we are asking more of classroom teachers, we are asking more of specialists as well, particularly those who teach students with disabilities in the content areas at the secondary level. Major efforts that build the instructional and attitudinal capacities of all teachers to work successfully with all students must accompany any effort to unify school systems. The capacity of the teaching staff to respond to all students must be at the core of any program evaluation.

The High Cost of Special Education

Separate systems are cumbersome and expensive. They are often more expensive than unified systems because the district is essentially required to duplicate many services, functions, and personnel resources. The public schools that offer a dual system consequently experience duplicative expense for the entire school budget. A historical lack of fulfillment of the funding promises made by legislators for the constellation of state and federal programs has resulted in calls for cost containment and a means to address the demands on shrinking general education budgets. Common public perception is that the greater piece of the educational pie is being invested in a particular group of students and the perception of some vocal critics is that too many dollars are being spent on students who are least likely to succeed.

The Process of Evaluation

The most important questions for an evaluation team to consider, regardless of whether the team is internal or external, are these:

- What prompted the evaluation?
- Who requested or commissioned it? Why?
- What are the expected outcomes of the evaluation?

We have argued before that only after these and other focus questions are identified can a study be designed and implemented. The early part of the evaluation design seeks to gain meaning and specificity around these questions. The importance of aligning methodology of evaluation with the inquiry questions cannot be underestimated.

Evaluation is more than data collection. The steps of data analysis and interpretation are critical as well, to make appropriate sense of the data collected. We think we all too often collect and report data without proper respect for the process of sense-making by various audiences. Neglecting to anticipate multiple interpretations leaves the analysis to others.

We have always asked our contact person in the district to select an internal leadership group made up of teachers, administrators, parents, and community members to provide a perspective on the evaluation focus. We also use this group to gain entry into the schools and community, to identify key informants, to make sense of the data while we are collecting it, to validate the data to maximize credibility, and finally to promote the use of the evaluation findings. This internal leadership group helps to engender a commitment in the district and community to the implementation work ahead. This group also creates an informed political force to monitor the implementation plan and be a voice that expects results.

What Difference Has Our Evaluation Work Made?

How have professionals within districts undergoing studies informed or changed their practice as a result of working with us for reflection and counsel? An assessment of an evaluation process and report must serve to forge greater capacity at the school site and within the district. The client school system should expect to get feedback on its vision and mission and to better clarify the parameters that it uses to guide decision making. In CAS terms, the district will redefine the minimum specifications it needs to promote quality service goals for all children. It is especially important to emphasize that program evaluations should always have recommendations for both general and special education services, personnel, and programs. The client school system should expect the evaluation process to unfreeze the barriers to specific program initiatives and program practices. Finally, the program evaluation process should create positive energy and renewed interest in collaborative practice between and among staff, community members, the district office, and individual schools.

Some evaluations we have done carried with them few surprises, while in others we have seen major awakenings, shifts in personnel, and a real transformation of thinking. In selected cases, we have seen programs changed and independent autonomous work of professionals become collaborative work. In some cases, it took a matter of months to see a real change; in others, the process began with a year or two of incorporating and internalizing findings. We remain in touch with many of our schools and districts and appreciate their continuing to inform our work.

Evaluation and the Playhouse

To visit our theater metaphor once again, we will cast the evaluator as the critic, who experiences the play, perhaps more than once. She sits in various seats and walks around interviewing audience members as they, too, experience the performance, the individual players, and the collective effect. The critic writes the review and thereby generates interest in the play. Sometimes the interest is positive and congratulatory; sometimes, it is scathing, prompting rewrites, recasting, and more rehearsals. Often a play is written or directed to project some passion or purpose. Sometimes it achieves that goal and sometimes it does not. Sometimes the writer, director, and actors work in harmony. At other times, there is an obvious lack of synchrony. The evaluator as critic paints a portrait of where the play is as an enterprise—not where it might like to be.

10

A Reflection on Leadership

Local Leadership Counts

We have selected a number of concepts—learner-centered schools, complex adaptive systems, and unified systems—and suggested ways to use them to shape future discourse on diversity and learning in the public schools. We want to close our work with a discussion of leadership. We have witnessed from our district consultations, training, and program evaluation studies many examples of local leadership that have led to the creation of unified systems. From the five case studies we presented earlier, superintendents and central office administrators in charge of student services have advocated for a more inclusive school philosophy because of their concerns about equity, as well as their concerns about preparing a compassionate future electorate.

Most recently, we observed a local assistant superintendent argue before her board of education that the district's high expectations and a commitment to high quality teaching were the reasons why

179

students with learning disabilities scored higher on the new state assessments than typical students in neighboring school districts. This leader used the district's high expectations for all students and the commitment of the teaching staff to support individual student success as examples of ways that a unified system serves all students, in spite of her special education cooperative's and neighboring school districts' commitment to preserving a continuum of services discourse. She has no peers in her neighboring communities who support her direction. She is both courageous and wise in the culture of the system, as well as extremely adept at finding internal colleagues to share new strategies for differentiating instruction to further a more individualized learning opportunities for all students. She clearly has managed from the edge and has helped transform her school system based on the concepts introduced in this book.

Managing from the edge begins with making the arguments for change and its moral purpose. In the case of this leader, equity begins and ends for students with disabilities in their home schools that have teachers who collaborate in serving all students together to achieve the same high expectations. Access to a challenging and meaningful curriculum that is postschool oriented is the goal for all. In our view, the most important roles of school leaders are in leading their school community in a democratic dialogue about the purposes of schooling and facilitating support for students and teachers.

The School Leader as a Public Intellectual

In *Moral Leadership*, Sergiovanni (1992) argues that notions of skills and processes have dominated the discourse about leadership. Skills and processes can be learned, but they are not sufficient to create the kinds of schools we need to respond to societal demands for excellence and achievement to a higher standard. School leaders must also have a vision for teaching and learning that is derived from widely held values and ennobling social ideals. Sergiovanni provides an example in urban leader Diana Lam, new superintendent of the Providence, Rhode Island, School District: "To her the key qualities needed in school leadership are an understanding of how children and adults learn and keep on learning and the ability to build communities of learners" (p. 1). To our way of thinking, this vision of leadership requires that school leaders see themselves as educative and political pathfinders who stimulate cooperative efforts to provide valued social goods in schools and communities.

Leadership as it is currently discussed is a process in which leaders' behavior is justified by bureaucratic, psychological, or rational-technical authority. Leaders are expected to use prescribed methods to control the activities of people and organizations and to maximize efficiency and productivity. Leaders are supposed to do things right to ensure that the organization achieves its objectives (Sergiovanni, 1992). For school administrators, this approach means that approved modes of classroom control, instruction, and assessment are chosen for use by teachers and other school personnel in an effort to teach the prescribed curriculum to as many students as possible. The school leader's authority comes from her position in the school district hierarchy, from her skill at motivating and manipulating teachers and other school personnel, and from her ability to exploit research in curriculum, instruction, and assessment practices.

Much of the discussion about the roles of school administrators has focused on moving administrators from their status as managers of schools to a stance as instructional leaders. The impetus for these efforts has come from the need to emphasize the need for instructional improvement in schools. Though these efforts are laudable and necessary, they do not address the need for a reflective discussion about education in the school-community.

As an institution, education lacks an informed public expression of its purposes, needs, and processes. It also lacks connections to other institutions and agencies that address social issues. If education is to play a role in ameliorating problems of poverty, discrimination, violence, and cultural dissonance, its purposes, needs, and processes must be communicated to, and integrated with, the efforts of others who are committed to similar ends. Communities must come to understand schools' roles in social transformation and support educational programs that sustain and stimulate society's efforts to improve the lot of all its citizens. For education to assume these roles, administrators must act as educational statesmen and representatives in the community.

We argue that this position is the province of school leaders and that this new role requires an ongoing commitment to personal learning and change, just as our vision of education requires continuous organizational learning and change. In our view, the role of the school leader is to act as a *public intellectual*—a moral and intellectual teacher and guide who engages the school community in discourse about the purposes of schooling and the means to achieve those purposes. The school leader's role must evolve from that of manager and educational expert to one of democratic practitioner and advocate for social goods within the institution of education and the individual lives of children.

The term *practice* is often used to describe what professionals do on a daily basis that enables them to become proficient at their jobs. We argue that the complexity of an administrator's daily responsibilities and the purposes that those engaged in the field of educational administration intend to accomplish require that school leaders' working theories of leadership and administration need to be refashioned. We suggest that school leaders adopt the term *practice* as it is explained by MacIntyre (1984) to describe their work and its intents (Lashley, 1994). Understanding educational administration in this language leads us to promote the view that educational administrators who work in the new leadership context of public schools should practice as public intellectuals. As a new working theory of school leadership and educational administration, our understandings of administrators as public intellectuals reconstructs educational administration as political and educative advocacy for schools, learning, and social transformation.

A criticism of educational administrators that brings both the institutional view and the practitioner's view into focus at the same time is offered below. It helps us explain the contradictions that occur when an individual's work behavior does not achieve the purposes that he or she values or those that are set forth by institutions. For example, a director of special education's efforts to ensure that students are treated fairly (the internal good of equity) may be constrained by district policies (institutional arrangements) that require that uniform standards be applied regardless of circumstances. The case of disciplinary policies is, of course, an excellent illustration. The director may be fearful (i.e., lacking the virtue of courage) of losing his job (and the external goods it provides). The institution (the school district), on the other hand, may see the director's insistence on equity as disruptive to its goal of treating students equally while preserving their safety from dangerous students and thereby withstanding challenges on the grounds that the district provides arbitrary, capricious, or politically motivated differential treatment for students. Using Stout's (1988) stereoscopic lens brings the practitioner's efforts to enact equity into focus by sharpening our understanding of the personal and institutional interests with which these efforts interact.

A New Leadership Context for Schools

Educational administration has traditionally taken its understandings of leadership from the business community. Sergiovanni (1996) argues that schools are unique institutions and that business conceptions do not apply to their purposes, desired outcomes, or processes. When educators try out theories of leadership that have been passed to them and promised outcomes do not follow, they conclude that they either did not understand the theory or they did not implement it properly. Rarely do they challenge the theory or think about inventing a theory of leadership that fits those unique institutions called schools.

For this discussion, we need to describe leadership as it should be in schools; that is, we need to invent a theory of school leadership and educational administration that fits our conceptions about what schools mean to communities and how school leaders interact with the core technologies of schools—teaching and learning, curriculum development, and responsibility for results (see Sergiovanni, 1996)—to bring about the personal and social transformations that education is supposed to generate. Because leadership is exercised by a variety of educational practitioners and by others with interests in the school-community's functioning, we must also devise a language that describes how those who hold administrative positions exercise leadership as they fulfill their particular responsibilities. In this light, we offer the following definitions of school leadership and educational administration:

School leadership is advocating for teaching and learning by articulating and working to achieve a school-community's shared educational commitments. Educational administration is the practice of advocating for teaching and learning by mobilizing economic, political, social, and personal resources to articulate and achieve a school-community's shared educational commitments.

Leadership and administration are terms that are often used interchangeably. Even though the nature of leadership in schools is a matter of considerable discussion and debate, those persons who hold administrative positions are generally expected to have leadership responsibilities. When the democratic process in leadership is highly valued, teachers, parents, community members, and students exercise leadership in an empowered school context, because democracy and learning are thought to be inextricably linked. The school leader is vested with the dual responsibility of (a) ensuring that the school community identifies and explores its values continually and democratically and (b) generating actions that pursue the goals of the school community.

Persons who have traditionally practiced as administrators may or may not have exercised leadership. Leadership has been a characteristic that devolved to a person in the context in which he worked; that is, leadership has been perceived to be a personal attribute. Democratic schools require a different notion of leadership, one in which the school community is constantly reminded of its commitments and its possible futures through a continual, open dialogue. Leadership must become a communal attribute in which all community members share responsibility for discursive dialogue and action. Administrators play an important role in providing the inellectual impetus for the leadership discourse, and they are situated in the organization in positions that provide them access to the resources and power necessary to bring about actions that direct the school community toward its goals. The development of discourses to be promoted within a school-community needs to be explicit.

The new leadership context of schools calls for increased participation by teachers, parents, and community members in the school's operations and decision making. The purpose of empowering these constituencies is to make decisions at the point in the school organization where they have the most influence, to foster ownership of the school's purposes and activities, and to create accountability. The administrator's role in this new leadership context is to advocate for and communicate the school's purposes, to facilitate the use of resources and networks that help the school accomplish its purposes, and to ensure that accountability is an integral part of school deliberations. The enactment of democratic ideals is foundational to our new theory of administrative practice, and democratic ideals are often cited, but not clearly articulated, in the discourse on school leadership.

According to Reitzug (1998), democratic ideals include a concern for the rights of others and the common good, authenticity in relationships, relationships that emphasize joint responsibility, collective responsibility for all persons, collaborative work, inquiry and discourse as routine activities in work life, a concern for equity, access to and equal opportunity for involvement in governance, shared leadership, and leadership through action and critique. Understanding the implications these conceptions have for school leadership and administration requires that new vocabulary and professional frameworks be considered by school leaders as they practice. In this light, we offer a social practice language and framework from the work of MacIntyre (1984) as a means for engaging in discourse about school leadership and educational administration.

Educational Administration as a Social Practice

School administrators work within the social institution of education. They have goals and objectives for their work, some of which are personal and some of which are professional. The institution of education, through its governance by states and school districts, also has goals and objectives that it intends to accomplish. Conflict between the goals of education as an institution and the professional and personal goals of administrators occurs as efforts are made to improve education for all students. This conflict is exacerbated by the demands made on the limited resources assigned to education by the economic and political institutions delegated by society to create the social order. These conflicts have implications for the work of administrators, whose personal and professional goals are constantly, and sometimes simultaneously, furthered and hindered by the goals of educational institutions.

MacIntyre (1984) uses the term *social practice* to describe collective human endeavors. The elements of a social practice are (a) practitioners engaged in cooperative activity; (b) historical context; (c) internal goods, which are accomplished by achieving standards of excellence; (d) external goods, which are rewards that accrue to practitioners as a result of their work; and (e) institutional arrangements that support the existence of a practice within a social institution. MacIntyre (1984) defines a social practice as any coherent and complex form of socially established cooperative human activity through which goods internal to that form of activity are realized in the course of trying to achieve those standards of excellence which are appropriate to, and partially definitive of, that form of activity, with the result that human powers to achieve excellence, and human conceptions of the ends and goods involved are systematically extended. (p. 187)

An excellent example of a transforming practice is the movement of a student with disabilities into the public schools in 1975 under PL 94-142. Under that legislation, the continuum of services discourse was encoded, which preserved the option to educate students with disabilities outside the public schools if the provision of the least restricted environment was protected. Within 10 years, the concept of inclusion dominated the discourse of what constitutes appropriate education for students with disabilities. In 1992, McLaughlin and Warren offered a third discourse for consideration in their policy options monograph suggesting the concept of a unified system. In 1992, the Council of Administrators of Special Education built its agenda on the unified system policy option to influence the direction of special services locally. Lashley (1993) and Burrello, Lashley, and Van Dyke (1996) added to the policy options the concept of a learner-centered discourse that moved the conversation from school structures and processes to classroom and teacher and student roles in the learning setting. The favored discourse selected affects the definition of internal and external goods. The school as an institution corrupts individual values and influences the values practitioners put on the different discourses, which, in turn, provide incentives to keep things the way they are.

Internal goods are accomplished when practitioners act in ways that are congruent with commonly held professional value. Some internal goods of the practice of educational administration include caring for students, fostering learning, cultivating efficacy, and working with others to accomplish internal goods. Stout (1988) has argued that analysis of professional practices has often focused only on the internal goods that practitioners should pursue. Whereas these analyses do not give a full and clear picture of practices as they exist in schools, they do provide some understandings about the ideals toward which practitioners aspire. The degree to which administrators are connected to practitioners who achieve standards of excellence and their connection to the excellence discourse in educational administration and school leadership will play a large role in influencing administrators' professional behavior and therefore their interest in and accomplishment of internal goods.

A New Theory of School Leadership and Educational Administration

A practice is a socially constituted set of intentions and activities in which practitioners pursue internal goods (valued actions and aims expressed in the language of the practice) and external goods (material benefits that accrue to individuals as a result of their participation in practices and other productive activities). Internal goods are achieved by meeting the standards of excellence of the practice through virtuous practice. Practices are enacted in the context of the places and lives in which they occur. Practitioners act in concert with traditions, with practitioners who have extended the standards of excellence of the practice, and within the institutions that support their practices. Because practices rely on institutions for support, institutions must create arrangements that (a) distribute external goods to practitioners and (b) provide the resource infrastructure within which practice occurs. These arrangements can cause practitioners to focus their attention on the accumulation of external goods, thereby detracting from the pursuit of internal goods, or to become fixated on maintaining the infrastructure that supports them, which averts their focus from the accomplishment of internal goods.

Social criticism has often focused either on whether internal goods that are appropriate to practices are being accomplished by practitioners or on the external goods necessary to practitioners and institutional arrangements necessary to support practices within institutions (Stout, 1988). Focusing solely on internal goods ignores the effects that factors such as power, wealth, and status have on social practices. Focusing exclusively on external goods reduces practices to sets of rational-technical procedures. Hence, Stout (1988) suggests that MacIntyre's (1984) framework be used to provide a stereoscopic criticism of social practices. Such a criticism involves an analysis of the elements of social practices and their effects on the actions of practitioners. A stereoscopic social criticism, according to Stout, "brings social practices and institutions, internal and external goods, into a single frame" (p. 280).

MacIntyre's (1984) social practice framework allows us to conceptualize education administration so that we may consider how practitioners act within the contexts in which they are situated to accomplish internal goods through meeting standards of excellence of the practice. Practitioners' pursuit of what they believe ought to be of value in the practice is affected by institutional arrangements and the pursuit of external goods. A stereoscopic criticism reveals how the accomplishment of the internal goods of the practice is affected by the institutional arrangements made to support the practice. Because institutional arrangements must take into account the goods of other practices, institutional goals can conflict with the accomplishment of the internal goods of a practice.

MacIntyre's framework provides a vocabulary for describing what ought to be in the practice of educational administration. The framework also provides a mechanism for describing how practitioners act to pursue goods within the institution of education and how their actions are constrained and enabled by external goods and institutional arrangements. An administrative practitioner who uses the social practice language and framework in his practical thoughts and actions will soon realize how necessary it is that he understand his connections to the practice of educational administration, its traditions, and other practitioners. The practitioner must understand what the practice stands for, the bases on which standards of excellence are constructed, and how the virtues are embedded in practitioners' conceptions of excellence. He will also soon realize that the institutions that support his practice and its methods of allocating institutional resources as external goods will serve as stumbling blocks to his accomplishment of internal goods. To explicate this process further, let us consider the issue of high standards for all students and its implementation in states, school districts, and schools. Several states have enacted legislation and policies requiring that all students meet high standards of achievement, and many states have developed high-stakes testing that students must pass before they can graduate from high school or move from level to level or grade to grade. In addition, some states have tied monetary rewards for teachers to high scores on student tests, and a popular notion ties the principal's job to high test scores and other quantitative measures of student progress across the school. This approach is conveniently quantifiable and therefore simple enough to reduce to a legislative report, a television news or radio sound bite, or a newspaper article. These institutional arrangements are put into place to motivate teachers and administrators to change their practices so that students will in turn be motivated to score higher on standardized tests. The rationale, oft repeated in the press, is that a rising tide of expectations raises all (students') ships. This new educational homily (replacing "All children can learn") is rooted in the effective schools research correlate that stated that effective schools (i.e., those with high test scores) were characterized by high teacher expectations for student achievement.

As a result of the implementation of high standards policies and the accompanying testing mania, schools have become focused on measurable academics, and the curriculum has been narrowed to include those facts and concepts that are tested by the state-administered assessment system. One need not do much more research than talking to school personnel in states such as New York, Indiana, Texas, and North Carolina to understand that teachers and administrators feel the pressure that these efforts bring to bear on them and their students. Whereas many educators recognize the good that high standards represent, they also recognize that other goods historically associated with American education are jeopardized by the emphasis on high test scores and the pressure placed on schools to generate them. For example, school people recognize that not all students learn at the same rate or in the same style and that instruction should respond to the needs of students; that is, they recognize that diversity is both inherent in students and an asset that educators should acknowledge. However, their pursuit of this good is constrained by the high test scores that institutional arrangements and the pressure on the security of their external goods impose. In this case, an institutional goal contravenes an internal good of educators, and the institutional arrangements force teachers to ignore their pursuit of diversity. Pursuing the good of diversity requires zealous—some would say foolish—exercise of the virtue of courage. Is it any wonder that educators lose hope when they are confronted with such political sophistry?

As with the case of high-standards policies, when we are faced with a social problem to solve—as complex as educating all children or as seemingly simple as teaching a child to read—we respond by turning to the literature to find a solution. What we find there is typified by what Karl Popper calls "holistic social engineering" (Havel, 1995, p. 3), or the appeal to theories and models of practice based on social laws that purport to circumscribe, control, and predict human affairs. This perspective comes from our grounding as 20th-century Americans in Enlightenment science and philosophy, Newtonian physics, and functionalist sociology (Wheatley, 1992), which posit an objective reality, subject-object dualism, and universal orderliness. Our hope under this conceptualization is to have one set of educational approaches that we can assemble, activate, and automate. High-standards policies certainly fit this bill because they attempt to apply one law of motivation to all students regardless of the circumstances under which their learning has occurred.

As educators, we recognize that the problems we are charged with solving are inherently subjective, highly complex and integrated, and chaotic. Our solutions are temporary at best and rarely have we found one approach that works in all situations. What we need, according to Havel (1995), is an approach that is grounded in "whatever has proved to be good, practical, desirable, and meaningful" (p. 3). This is not to say that we should rely on that which is expedient or that which simply works. Rather, educators should engage in a "critical pragmatism" (Cherryholmes, 1988), in which we continuously examine approaches that are of use in the short term to determine whether they are helping us achieve our democratic ideals. For example, placing students with disabilities in separate classes "worked" in the sense that the responsibility for these children was given to specialists and the burden of their instruction was removed from general educators. However, upon examination (Brantlinger, 1998; Skrtic, 1991), this workable solution has been found to violate democratic ideals such as equity, equal opportunity, concern for the rights of others, and collective responsibility. More pertinent, it has precluded general educators from learning how to assume responsibility for students with disabilities, thereby creating both logistical and psychological obstacles to students' return to the regular classroom.

To have a system that is grounded in goodness *and* practicality (i.e., a critical and pragmatic system) and that responds to the diversity that marks the educational landscape, school leaders who speak out on the educational and social issues of the day must become advocates for their practices. They must practice as public intellectuals who see it as their responsibility to educate their school-communities, their constituents, and their fellow professionals about the crucial importance of education to a democratic society. Whereas business and social engineering consultants have popularized the management guru and visionary as role models for school leaders, education is a significantly different enterprise that requires a simultaneously practical and theoretical discussion about what to do and how to do it. The school leader's role in this discourse is to organize resources to facilitate practitioner access to ideas and to create occasions for discourse to occur.

According to Havel (1995), an intellectual is "a person who has devoted his or her life to thinking in general terms about the affairs of this world and the broader context of things. . . . their [sic] principal occupation is studying, reading, teaching, writing, publishing, addressing the public" (p. 3). Intellectuals "perceive the broader context . . . [have an] . . . increased sense of responsibility for this world . . . build people-to-people solidarity . . . [and] . . . wage a struggle for every good thing" (p. 4). Intellectuals know how their practices fit into the greater scheme of things, and they feel responsible to make a difference. They become public intellectuals when they take public stances and make efforts to inform the public about issues that are important to the common good.

Public intellectuals address the problems of society. Educational public intellectuals engage in social criticism and foster educational discourse that brings schools into the public sphere. They discuss, understand, and promote the role that education plays in the continual renewal of civic virtue and responsible citizenship. They resist the corrupting influences that institutions and external goods play in practitioners' efforts to realize the promise that the internal goods have for students, communities, and democratic society.

The call here is for a public intellectual to take up the critical project and its sophisticated analysis of society and culture. Public intellectuals use their knowledge to create new vocabularies and frameworks that emphasize notions of ethics, power, personal agency, and the common good. They merge theory and discourse to construct practices, policies, and programs that address important social problems and foster democratic participation as their central task. Educators have a crucial role to play in this discourse, and they, of all professionals, are effectively situated to provide both abstract and concrete examples of the effects of institutional arrangements on the pursuit of social goods, the deleterious influence that competition and disproportionate distribution of external goods has on society, and the consequences of our lack of consideration of citizenship, responsibility, and long-term thinking have on the environment and the social fabric.

Administrative Theory and Practice in the New Leadership Context

Education is at a low point in its prestige as a profession. The educational system, as it is currently arranged, is thought to be the problem in American society rather than a solution. The solutions that are offered by most legislative and business interests rely on assumptions and intentions that are antithetical to the internal goods that educators have valued in their practices. Goods that are rooted in the American tradition, such as equity, citizenship, tolerance, flexibility, and democracy, have been overshadowed by competitiveness, productivity, standardization, accumulation of wealth, and personal well-being. Society values education for the contribution it makes to economic development, not for its critical contributions to social justice, personal growth, and community progress. Certainly, economic development is an important component of a vital society, but it is not the only purpose that marks a good society nor is it sufficient reason to educate children.

If education is to assume its rightful place as an institution that participates in the creation of a moral, just, and courageous society, then educators must assert themselves not only as instructors of children but as representatives of the American tradition in which citizens speak out about issues that are critical to social growth. We contend that educational administrators are in the proper positions to represent education in the broader social discourse. Administrators must think, read, write, and speak about issues that children face and the roles that schools play in a democratic society. They must act in ways that are resonant of community values and that challenge injustice, inequity, dishonesty, and cowardice when schools are criticized for their advocacy on behalf of children, families, and communities. In sum, educational administrators must become public intellectuals who lead social discourse as it relates to educating the citizenry for participation in the good society.

As public intellectuals, administrative practitioners are responsible for seeing that the school's activities occur in alignment with values that represent a consensus of the school-community. They must work constantly to be sure that the collective values of the school are regularly and openly examined and articulated, that the values are communicated to the school's publics, and that the publics have the opportunity to understand and influence the school's activities and values. The process of leading public discourse requires that the administrator have the knowledge, skills, and dispositions necessary to see that power flows freely among the school's publics and constituencies and that resources are pursued and accessed to enable the school to undertake activities that are central to its mission. The school administrator also has the responsibility to ensure that the school and its constituencies are accountable for their actions as they relate to the educational, social, and political missions of the school.

Recently in New York and Michigan, we have witnessed the commitment of selected school superintendents to redefine what they mean by school success. They are entering the discourse on accountability and student success in response to the arbitrary and capacious nature of state testing standards that reduce the meaning of school career to a 2-day test for 10th- or 11th-grade students. These superintendents are preparing responses that illustrate the double standard that states are using to measure selected minimal graduation competency and advanced proficiencies in the same test, while neglecting the support and attention necessary to bring the diversity of our student populations to either standard.

These superintendents' stances as public intellectuals represent a very different role for school administrators, who are used to managing the status quo and avoiding controversy. Preparing and selecting school administrators to assume this role will require that persons who are motivated by ideas such as justice, equity, and democracy be attracted to administration and that their lifelong education be oriented toward understanding cultural criticism and the political nature of their work. This kind of preparation will require a quantum shift in both their academic preparation and their engagement with ideas during their careers. Although understanding curriculum and instruction and what it is like to be a teacher will be important for administrators, articulating that knowledge in the context of its contribution to the community will be the most important responsibility they have.

The School as Playhouse

In this chapter we have attempted to provide a framework for a new theory of educational administration in which administrators practice as public intellectuals. Although we recognize that this shift is dramatic and fraught with uncertainty for educators and communities, we believe it is critical if education is to be an important factor in realizing the dream set forth in the American experiment. We use the metaphor of the school as a playhouse to illustrate our theory and its usefulness in reconstructing education as a democratic project:

In our conception of the school as playhouse, a school principal practices like a director. She is responsible for recruiting and preparing the cast, providing an overview and blocking out cast members' work, coordinating their efforts, and generally providing the intellectual and technical framework within which the play will occur. The cast consists of teachers and other employees, who act as veteran performers, and students, who are novice performers and members of the chorus getting much-needed experience.

The principal coordinates the resources that have been made available to her by district administrators, who are practicing in their capacities as producers. District-level administrators, such as directors of special services are charged with providing support, both through provision of resources and by serving as advocates for a particular vision of what the production is to become. Directors of special services are responsible to see that the needs and interests of students with disabilities and other special needs receive the attention they deserve as the production proceeds. The director of special services works closely with the principal to ensure that resources are used well and that they serve appropriate purposes.

The principal must keep the purpose of the play—the moral of the story—together and ensure that the script moves along coherently. This requires that she communicate with members of the cast about the ideas they are trying to get across to the audience. She must simultaneously manipulate resources and shelter the cast from those manipulations to ensure that their energies stay focused on the task of understanding and interpreting the script so that all of its intricacy is appreciated by all concerned. She must also be a critic—one who points out the improper assumptions and inconsistencies that cast members are including in their portrayal of characters. The principal's practice is oriented toward presenting a yearlong performance that stimulates learning and prepares teachers to get the most from their roles and students to move on to other roles. The principal also speaks to the public about the work in progress and stimulates its interest in both the play as an event and the play's importance in society.

While the principal is staging her yearlong production, the director of special services is organizing resources to continue the support of that production and arranging for new productions. He is advocating with executive producers (superintendents) and boards of directors (boards of education) for more resources that address the issues about which he is professionally concerned. He, too, is acting as a critic, providing feedback to principals and teachers about the reactions of parents, policymakers, and other agencies to the production underway and is speaking publicly about the needs of students with disabilities and special needs to garner further support and to stem the droves of naysayers who would stop the production's efforts on behalf of these students.

As she practices, the principal draws on her own experiences and the experiences of other practitioners who have gone before her. She activates the bonds between cast members and the community that make the play meaningful and successful. She also serves as the school's conscience, providing encouragement and feedback, augmenting good work and remedying problems, and holding forth on the aims and purposes the cast intends to accomplish. Because of the principal's leadership, the school year is more than a collection of technical actions strung together over time. It becomes a set of purposeful activities from which students, teachers, the community, and the principal learn, grow, and prosper.

While the principal is holding forth on the educational front lines, gathering both blame and glory, the director of special services is working behind the scenes to improve the likelihood that the production will continue to serve all students. The director is attending to the institutional arrangements necessary to ensure that principals and teachers have what they need to do their work—unglamorous work to be sure, but necessary for the show to go on. The director balances this side of her work life—the paperwork, the professional bureaucracy, the community meetings—with a strongly held belief in the internal goods of her practice: equity, justice, caring. Although it is easy to become jaded when she is faced with lack of support, scarce resources, and mounds of busywork, the moral foundation on which her practice is built must be strong to encourage her to persevere.

That moral foundation more frequently comes to the forefront of her practice when others (administrators, policymakers, parents, members of the community) express views that are antithetical to the director's professional purposes. In a democratic community, it is the director's job and moral responsibility to ensure that the political dialogue about education includes the interests of students with disabilities and special needs. Society, through its elected officials, has determined that these students will equitably participate in all educational productions. When other players stray from that path, the director of special services has a responsibility to stand up for these students. In that respect, s/he is the moral compass by which the school district can determine its direction. His/her compass points are the internal goods of the practice of educating all students of the community.

Resources

A. Case Studies of Special Education Leadership and Programs and Services

B. Program Evaluation Self-Study Guide: Leading School Systems, Program Components and/or School-Site Appraisal Efforts

Resource A Case Studies of Special Education Leadership and Programs and Services

Community Context	Students	Teachers	Leadership	Community Members
Northeast—a primarily middle-class community with a large proportion of professional patrons.	Self-referenced assessment where competition is reduced between students, and personal responsibility for planning and carrying out personal plans are emphasized. Where all students have a personal plan developed with their parents and teachers.	All teachers are facilitators of individual student plans and share in the education of a multiage cohort of students with their colleagues. Teachers are active inquirers, using data from student projects and their own observations as a means of inviting parents to learn and support their child's learning performance. Special support teachers are an integral part of the teaching cohort team.	Preoccupied with quality and the measurement of learning on the part of teachers. Expected teachers to invite students to design and implement their independent learning plans in a collaborative or social learning setting. Leadership focuses on getting community support for student empowerment and helping parents learn to help their children succeed.	Community resisted movement to student empowerment until it was demonstrated to their satisfaction that their children exceed state norms of performance. They requested and required the school leadership to provide data and frequent communication on matters related to the curriculum and local and state assessments. Parents are invited weekly to assess their child's personal best and codesign their child's individual learning plan and evaluate it quarterly.

Community Context	Students	Teachers	Leadership	Community Members
Eastern seaboard—a primarily working-class community with a full range of professional and technically employed patrons.	Adults are responsible for planning and delivery of a traditional elementary and high school curriculum. Low tolerance for acting-out behavior.	Special services staff had no discernible standards for student achievement. Their goal for students was for them to fit in and not cause trouble. Union bargaining agreement struck in 1970s. Clearly teacher-centered schools; little to no evidence of collaboration.	Special services leadership driven by compliance standards in state and federal rules and regulations. Top leadership held hostage by special education interpretation of regulations, and seen as the court of last resort on student behavior. No evidence of programming of in-district services to students with severe behavioral problems. Significant budget overruns an annual event.	Parents held a more contemporary and inspiring vision of student possibilities than the district leadership. Well-informed parents who fought the district got relief for their children and more inclusive educational opportunities. Major community segments concerned about the costs of special services and their impinging on services for their children. Little to no community education program in place for parents of students with disabilities or for typical parents about the needs of special-need students.

(continued)

Community Context	Students	Teachers	Leadership	Community Members
Northeastern urban setting—a diverse, well-informed, cosmopolitan city with an active social conscience.	All students with special needs and English as a second language (ESL) included in age-appropriate school settings.	Special services staff competent in assessment, case management, and rule compliance; however, not very good at interpreting the curriculum, collaboration, and adapting instruction to the typical classroom. Role erosion was a frequently cited concern.	High-touch, special education leadership, very much site-managed, with top- and school-level leadership support. Top leadership finding ways to include special education assessment of student progress in district strategy plan report. Role of special education staff still distinct at the school level, which confounds implementation of the district's unified system vision held by top leadership. District leadership committed to equity and high student performance across schools.	Well-informed community, actively involved in school affairs. Little concern about equity in student access to services across schools. Major community concerns about failing students at high school and students of poverty impacting two elementary schools.

Community Context	Students	Teachers	Leadership	Community Members
Midwest—a suburban neighbor to a highly impacted urban school district. Very racially and ethnically conscious district with high community involvement.	Growing special needs population as competition heats up. Middle and high schools less hospitable to students with disabilities (SWD).	High academic orientation. Uses a case management model, with instructional aides providing much of the direct services to SWD in inclusive classrooms. Secondary special education teachers losing sense of their role.	Leadership very aware and sensitive to quality reputation for services to all students. Pioneer in services to SWD and many leading examples of successful inclusion. Dilemma exists over how to change the delivery system without losing community support. In search of alternatives. Service delivery models without litigation following changes.	Community well-educated and demanding of quality services. Sought-out community because of its schools and their reputation. Values diversity but not at the cost of quality.

(continued)

Community Context	Students	Teachers	Leadership	Community Members
Southwest—a suburban neighbor to a highly impacted urban school district. Very racially and ethnically conscious district with high community involvement. A district in transition.	Growing special needs population as competition heats up. Middle and high schools less hospitable to students with disabilities.	High academic orientation. Uses special class and instructional resource model in providing much of the direct services to SWD. Spotty examples of inclusive classrooms. Teachers contend they are taking their marching orders from their regular class counterparts. Very little evidence of professional development and alternatives to current models in place.	Leadership very aware of and sensitive to quality reputation for services to all students. Few examples of inclusive practices evident. Dilemma exists over how to change the delivery system without losing community support. Litigation following changes is a primary fear, along with how to develop safeguards to protect students' and parents' rights. New leadership drawn from regular education came about after a negative special education study was in the offing. New leadership committed to create alternatives and maintain top leadership and community support. Chief challenge: high school principals and their athletic fiefdoms.	Community well-educated and demanding of quality services. Sought-out community because of its schools and proximity to urban center. Little tolerance for ambiguity and lack of consistency in interpretation of services. Demanding equity across schools.

Resource B Program Evaluation Self-Study Guide
Leading School Systems, Program Components and/or School-Site Appraisal Efforts
Developed by Leonard C. Burrello and Edith E. Beatty

	Current Practice	Gap Between Desired Practice and Current Practice	Rating (1-10)	Data Source(s)
Vision, Governance, and Policy				
Shared Mind-Set				
To what extent does the district or school site have a vision and a set of core values to enforce its practice				
To what extent does the current culture support the district vision and mission?				
Governance/Policy				
To what extent does the district or school have the right organizational structure to support alternative service delivery systems or options?				
To what extent do the district's communication and problem-solving processes and policies support a particular discourse on special services?				

(continued)

	Current Practice	Gap Between Desired Practice and Current Practice	Rating (1-10)	Data Source(s)

Specific Policy Issues

To what extent are policies aligned with a continuum of service, inclusion, or a unified system direction for special education, 504, or Title I services?

To what extent are policies aligned with state and federal regulations?

To what extent do policies indicate a commitment to equity and inclusion of all students?

Leadership and Management

Leadership

To what extent does the district or school have the leadership to achieve its goals?

To what extent are district or school leaders agreed on a common agenda inclusive of students with special needs?

To what extent is the leadership, including teacher-leaders, committed to a unified system of quality education for all students?

	Current Practice	Gap Between Desired Practice and Current Practice	Rating (1-10)	Data Source(s)
To what extent does the leadership involve students and parents in planning and problem solving around issues that concern them?				
To what extent are leaders committed to achieving high expectations for all students?				
To what extent is there an organizational focus on system change and school-level development and accountability for results in student performance?				
To what extent is the leadership a key force in community education, involving community agencies and institutions of higher education to provide services and programs to students, families, and staff?				
Management				
To what extent is district management committed to school site management?				

(continued)

	Current Practice	Gap Between Desired Practice and Current Practice	Rating (1-10)	Data Source(s)
Can school teams make decisions about programs and service models and resource allocations including personnel, school improvement plans, and professional development?				
To what extent are there communication and problem-solving procedures in place to deal with emerging needs, issues, events, and parent and advocate complaints?				
To what extent is there an ongoing negotiating process to support changes in the special needs population school by school?				
To what extent is the management information structure from case managers to district supervisors appropriate and efficient to meet the information requirements to support student performance, referral, identification and evaluation, and student educational planning and placement to meet local, state, and federal reporting needs?				

	Current Practice	Gap Between Desired Practice and Current Practice	Rating (1-10)	Data Source(s)
Intellectual Capital/Competence				
Intellectual Capital				
To what extent has the district or school been successful in attracting, developing, and retaining individuals committed to personalizing education for all students, taking advantage of emerging technologies to individualize instruction, and able to develop and share their knowledge to create a learning organization at their school?				
Competence				
To what extent does the district or school have the required knowledge, skills, and abilities to serve its unique school population?				
To what extent is professional development, consistent with the five principles of effectiveness, evident at the school site?				

(continued)

	Current Practice	Gap Between Desired Practice and Current Practice	Rating (1-10)	Data Source(s)
—building based				
—using coaching and other follow-up procedures				
—collaborative				
—embedded in the daily lives of teachers, providing for continuous growth				
—focused on student learning and is evaluated in part on that criterion				
To what extent is staff development focused on the development of skills that enable teachers and support staff to effectively teach all students?				
To what extent are there systematic relationships between district direction, standards and goals, programs and services, evaluation data, and action plans that tighten alignment between the elements of an effective delivery system?				

	Current Practice	Gap Between Desired Practice and Current Practice	Rating (1-10)	Data Source(s)
Developing and Improving the Education Program for All Students				
To what extent are quality standards and high expectations established for all students?				
To what extent are opportunities provided for all students to participate in the district's core curriculum?				
To what extent are outcomes appropriate for all students with disabilities?				
To what extent is participation in the general education facilitated for students with disabilities to ensure equal access?				
To what extent are teaching styles and learning environments responsive to students' cultures, behavior, and learning styles?				
To what extent are individual student learning styles accommodated to ensure success in core curriculum activities in the general education environment?				

(continued)

	Current Practice	Gap Between Desired Practice and Current Practice	Rating (1-10)	Data Source(s)
To what extent are flexible grouping practices used to promote fluidity, diversity appreciation, and cooperative learning?				
To what extent is continual assessment, using multiple data sources, used for program planning and decision making?				
To what extent are program objectives and activities focused on student outcomes?				
To what extent are the best instructional practices based on research and evaluation data?				
To what extent do students with disabilities receive instruction in age-appropriate facilities with their nondisabled peers for the same length of time as the general education students with access to the same curriculum?				

	Current Practice	Gap Between Desired Practice and Current Practice	Rating (1-10)	Data Source(s)
To what extent is a systematic method used to track students as they transfer from one school, level, or program to another, including postsecondary involvement?				
To what extent is current research used to improve program effectiveness?				
To what extent are data on individual students being used to assess progress in the general education curriculum?				
To what extent are adapted or functional curricula available for students with more significant disabilities?				
To what extent does instruction support the transfer of training to nonschool environments?				
To what extent are prereferral intervention strategies systematically used to enhance student performance and support a preventive approach?				

(continued)

211

	Current Practice	Gap Between Desired Practice and Current Practice	Rating (1-10)	Data Source(s)
To what extent are prevention activities and programs monitored at the building level to ensure student progress or success according to specified guidelines and procedures?				
To what extent does the district hold itself accountable?				
Preschool Programming				
To what extent are early identification or intervention services provided through school and community resources for children and their families?				
To what extent do cooperative or collaborative arrangements exist between community-based preschools, day care centers, Head Start programs and the public schools; and how do these arrangements facilitate the provision of early intervention services to young children and their families?				

	Current Practice	Gap Between Desired Practice and Current Practice	Rating (1-10)	Data Source(s)
To what extent are early primary (infancy-Grade 3) programs flexible enough to meet an array of students' developmental needs in regard to facilities, space, and curriculum?				
To what extent is a viable communication process in place for transmitting information from private or community early childhood programs to public school programs to ensure smooth transitions and program continuity for students entering school-age programs?				
Transitional Programming				
To what extent has a written, comprehensive, transition plan been developed for all students with disabilities, age 14 or older?				
To what extent do adult service providers and community agency representatives actively participate in the transition planning process?				

(continued)

	Current Practice	Gap Between Desired Practice and Current Practice	Rating (1-10)	Data Source(s)
To what extent does transition planning address: preparation for employment, postsecondary education, and arrangements for independent living?				
To what extent are preventive intervention plans and transitional services coordinated with various professionals and community agencies to ensure a unified approach?				
Technology				
To what extent are instructional technologies integrated into the curriculum?				
To what extent do students have access to appropriate technology?				
To what extent is technology distributed rather than centralized in labs?				
To what extent are teachers trained in the use of technology?				
To what extent do teachers have access to technology for planning and reporting purposes?				

	Current Practice	Gap Between Desired Practice and Current Practice	Rating (1-10)	Data Source(s)
To what extent are instructional opportunities for students with special needs enhanced by assistive technologies?				
To what extent are teachers or support staff trained to use assistive devices?				
Developing and Maintaining the Educational Climate and the Learning Environment				
To what extent do students perceive teachers as caring and involving students in planning and evaluating their school work?				
To what extent does the school staff promote and use the family educational culture as a resource to encourage student bonding with education and their school?				
To what extent is the school safe and accessible to all students, including those with special mobility needs, and their parents?				

(continued)

	Current Practice	Gap Between Desired Practice and Current Practice	Rating (1-10)	Data Source(s)
To what extent are school staff trained to manage behavior and crisis situations for students with specialized behavioral or health needs?				
Developing and Involving the Community of Stakeholders				
To what extent is community involvement and decision making evident at the district and school level?				
To what extent are parents partners in their children's educational plan?				
To what extent are parents satisfied with the school's programs and services?				
To what extent are community patrons satisfied with the school's programs and services?				
To what extent have parents grieved and complained about school programs and services?				
How have those complaints been resolved?				
To what extent does the district or individual school have data on parent and community satisfaction?				

	Current Practice	Gap Between Desired Practice and Current Practice	Rating (1-10)	Data Source(s)
Developing and Monitoring Fiscal Resources				
To what extent are resources merged to support an integrated service delivery system for all students?				
To what extent are resources allocated equity across the district and schools to ensure equal access for all students?				
To what extent are district and school-level expenditures for special-needs students appropriately allocated and expended for their intended purposes?				
To what extent are the school-site profiles that are built and revised annually used to guide the negotiation of resources?				
To what extent are cost studies done to assess the benefit of particular program interventions to student needs?				
Performance Orientation and Consequences				
Performance Orientation				
To what extent is there a performance orientation to measure student achievement and access to the general education standards and goals for all students?				

(continued)

217

	Current Practice	Gap Between Desired Practice and Current Practice	Rating (1-10)	Data Source(s)
To what extent are alternative standards and performance criteria used for students with significant learning needs?				
To what extent are students included in all statewide assessments?				
To what extent are multiple assessment devices (portfolio, exhibitions) being used to assess student progress?				
Is authentic learning occurring?				
To what extent are modifications and accommodations available to assist students with special needs to participate in statewide assessments?				
To what extent are data desegregated to illustrate the effect of separate interventions on students with special needs?				
To what extent is student performance documented and shared with students and their parents or guardians?				

	Current Practice	Gap Between Desired Practice and Current Practice	Rating (1-10)	Data Source(s)
Consequences To what extent does the district or school have the appropriate rewards and incentives to support student and staff learning and growth opportunities?				
To what extent are multiple program assessments by district or school used to change, modify, or discontinue a practice?				
To what extent does the district or school use action plans to improve work processes, to change, and to learn?				
Capacity for Change To what extent does the district or school have the ability to improve work processes, to change, and to learn?				

References

American Psychological Association. (1995). *Learner-centered principles: A framework for school redesign and school organization.* Denver, CO: Love.

Barker, J. (1986). *Discovering the future: The business of paradigms* [Videotape]. Burnsville, MN: Charthouse.

Branson. R. (1987). Why the schools can't improve: The upward limit hypothesis. *Journal of Instructional Development, 10*(4), 15-26.

Brantlinger, E. (1997). Using ideology: Cases of non-recognition of the politics of research and practice in special education. *Review of Educational Research, 67,* 425-459.

Brown, A., & Campione, J. (1990). Communities of learning and thinking, or a context by any other name. *Human Development, 21,* 108-125.

Brown, A., & Campione, J. (1996). Psychological theory and the design of innovative learning environment: On procedures, principles, and systems. In L. Chauble & R. Glaser (Eds.), *Innovations in learning: New environments for education.* Mahwah, NJ: Lawrence Erlbaum.

Brown, A., & Campione, J. (1998). Designing a community of learners. In N. Lambert & B. McCombs (Eds.), *How students learn: Reforming schools through learner-centered education.* Washington, DC: American Psychological Association.

Bruner, J. (1963). *The process of education.* Cambridge, MA: Harvard University Press.

Bulgren, J. A., Deshler, D. D., & Schumaker, J. B. (1993). *The concept mastery routine.* Lawrence, KS: Edge.

Bulgren, J. A., Lenz, B. K., Schumaker, J. B., & Deshler, D. D. (1995). *The use and effectiveness of a concept comparison routine in secondary-level mainstream classes.* Lawrence: University of Kansas Center for Research on Learning.

Bulgren, J. A., Schumaker, J. B., & Deshler, D. D. (1994a). *The concept anchoring routine*. Lawrence, KS: Edge.

Bulgren, J. A., Schumaker, J. B., & Deshler, D. D. (1994b). The effects of a recall enhancement routine on the test performance of secondary students with and without learning disabilities. *Learning Disabilities Research & Practice, 9*(1), 2-11.

Burrello, L. (Producer). (1996). *For our students, for ourselves* [Videocassette]. (Available from the Forum on Education, Indiana University, Bloomington, IN.)

Burrello, L. (Producer). (1999). *Reaching for the North Star* [Videocassette]. Bloomington: Indiana University, Forum on Education.

Burrello, L., & Lashley, C. (1992). The destiny of special education. In K. Waldron, A. Riester, & J. Moore (Eds.), *Special education in the future.* San Francisco: Mellen Research University Press.

Burrello, L., Lashley, C., & Van Dyke, R. (1996). Aligning job accountability standards in a unified system of education. *Special Education Leadership Review, 3*(1), 29-41.

Burrello, L., Tracy, M. L., & Schultz, E. (1973). Special education as experimental education. *Exceptional Children, 38*, 29-33.

Burrello, L. & Zadnik, D. (1986). Critical success factors of special education administrators. *Journal of Special Education, 20*(3), 367-377.

Cherryholmes, C. H. (1988). *Power and criticism: Poststructuralist investigations in education.* New York: Teachers College Press.

Clinton, W. J. (1999). *State of the union address.* Washington, DC: The White House.

Collins, J., & Porras, J. (1996, September-October,). Building your company's vision. *Harvard Business Review*, 65-78.

Cook, L., & Friend, M. (1995). Co-teaching: Guidelines for creating effective practices. *Focus on Exceptional Children, 28*(3), 1-16.

Cook, L., & Friend, M. (1996). Co-teaching: Guidelines for creating effective practices. In Meyen, E., Vergason, G., & Whelan, R. *Strategies for teaching exceptional children in inclusive settings.* Denver, CO: Love.

Council of Administrators of Special Education (CASE), Inc. (1992). *Future agenda.* Albuquerque, NM: Author.

Covey, S. R. (1989). *The seven habits of highly successful people: Restoring the character ethic.* New York: Simon & Schuster.

Darling-Hammond, L. (1993). Reframing the school reform agenda: Developing capacity for school transformation. *Phi Delta Kappan, 74*(10), 753-761.

Darling-Hammond, L. (1997). *The right to learn: A blueprint for creating schools that work.* San Francisco: Jossey-Bass.

Davis, S., & Botkin, J. (1994). *The monster under the bed.* New York: Touchstone.

Delquadri, J. C., Greenwood, C. R., Stretton, K., & Hall, R. V. (1983). The peer tutoring spelling: A classroom procedure for increasing opportunity to respond and spelling performance. *Education and Treatment of Children, 6*(3), 225-239.

Delquadri, J. C., Greenwood, C. R., Whorton, D., Carta, J. J., & Hall, R. V. (1986). Classwide peer tutoring. *Exceptional Children, 52*(6), 535-542.

Deno, E. N. (1970). Special education as developmental capital. *Exceptional Children, 37,* 299-340.

Deshler, D. D., & Schumaker, J. B. (1988). An instructional model for teaching students how to learn. In J. E. Zins & M. J. Curtis (Eds.), *Alternative educational delivery system: Enhancing instructional options for all students.* Washington, DC: National Association of School Psychologists.

Dewey, J. (1902). *The child and the curriculum.* Chicago: University of Chicago Press.

Ebeling, D., Deschenes, C., & Sprague, J. (1994). *Adapting curriculum and instruction in inclusive classrooms: A teacher's desk guide.* Bloomington, IN: Institute for the Study of Developmental Disabilities, Center for School and Community Integration.

Edmonds, R. (1979). Effective schools for the urban poor. *Educational Leadership, 37,* 15-32.

Elkind, D. (1989). Developmentally appropriate practice: Philosophical and practical implications. *Phi Delta Kappan, 71*(2), 113-117.

Elmore, R. F. (1996). Getting to scale with good educational practice. *Harvard Educational Review, 66*(1), 1-26.

Ettinger, L. (1999, May). *Complex adaptive systems: Building a unified system.* Paper presented at the Forum on Education, UCEA Center on Special Education & Department of Education, State of Indiana Conference.

Fetterman, D. M., Kaftarian, S. J., & Wandersman, A. (Eds.). (1996). *Empowerment evaluation.* Thousand Oaks, CA: Sage.

Fisher, J., Schumaker, J., & Deshler, D. (1996). Searching for validated inclusive practices: A review of the literature. In E. Meyen, G. Vergason, & R. Whelan (Eds.), *Strategies for teaching exceptional children in inclusive settings.* Denver, CO: Love.

Friend, M., & Bursuch, W. (1996). *Including students with special needs: A practical guide for classroom teachers.* Boston: Allyn & Bacon.

Fullan, M. (1991). *The new meaning of educational change.* New York: Teachers College Press.

Fullan, M. (1994). *Change forces: Probing the depths of educational reform.* Bristol, PA: Falmer.

Fullan, M. (1995). The limits and the potential of professional development. In T. R. Guskey & M. Huberman (Eds.), *Professional development in education: New paradigms and practices.* New York: Teachers College Press.

Fullan, M. (1998). Breaking the bonds of dependency. *Educational Leadership,* 55(7), 1-10.

Gardner, H. (1987). *Frames of mind: The theory of multiple intelligence.* New York: Basic Books.

Garmston, R., & Wellman, B. (1995). Adaptive schools in a quantum universe. *Educational Leadership, 52*(7), 6-13.

Gartner, A., & Lipsky, D. (1987). Beyond special education: Toward a quality system for all students. *Harvard Education Review, 57*(4), 367-395.

Gartner, A., & Lipsky, D. (1989). *The yoke of special education: How to break it.* Rochester, NY: National Center on Education and the Economy.

Goodlad. J. (1984). *A place called school.* New York: McGraw-Hill.

Greenwood, C. R., Delquadri, J. C., & Hall, R. V. (1984). Opportunity to respond and student academic performance. In W. L. Heward, T. E. Heron, J. Trap-Porter, & D. S. Hill (Eds.), *Focus on behavior analysis in education.* Columbus, OH: Merrill.

Gregory, T., & Smith, G. (1987). *High schools as communities: The small school reconsidered.* Bloomington, IN: Phi Delta Kappan.

Hamel, G., & Prahalad, C. K. (1994). *Competing for the future.* Boston: Harvard Business School Press.

Havel, V. (1995). The responsibilities of intellectuals. *New York Review of Books, 63*(11), 36.

Heifetz, R., & Laurie, D. (1997). The work of leadership. *Harvard Business Review,* (1/2), 124-134.

Higgins, K., & Boone, R. (1992). Hypermedia computer study guides for social studies: Adapting a Canadian history text. *Social Education, 56*(3), 154-159.

Horton, S. V., & Lovitt, T. C. (1989). Using study guides with three classifications of secondary students. *Journal of Special Education, 22*(4), 447-462.

Horton, S. V., Lovitt, T. C., & Bergerud, D. (1990). The effectiveness of graphic organizers for three classifications of secondary students in content area classes. *Journal of Learning Disabilities, 23*(1), 12-22.

Horton, S. V., Lovitt, T. C., Givens, A., & Nelson, R. (1989). Teaching social studies to high school students with academic handicaps in mainstream setting: effects of a computerized study guide. *Journal of Learning Disabilities, 22*(2), 102-107.

Horton, S. V., Lovitt, T. C., & Slocum, T. (1988). Teaching geography to high school students with academic deficits: Effects of a computerized map tutorial. *Learning Disability Quarterly, 11,* 371-379.

Hourcade, J., & Bauwens, J. (1996). Cooperative teaching: Levels of involvement. *Special Education Leadership Review, 3*(1), 57-63.

House, E. R. (1981). Three perspectives on innovation: Technical, political, and cultural. In R. Lehming, & M. Kane (Eds.), *Improving schools using what we know.* Beverly Hills, CA: Sage.

Howe, H. (1995). Uncle Sam is in the classroom. *Phi Delta Kappan, 76*(1), 374-377.

Idol, L. (1987). Group story mapping: A comprehensive strategy for both skilled and unskilled readers. *Journal of Learning Disabilities, 20*(4), 196-205.

Individuals With Disabilities Education Act Amendments of 1997, 20 U.S.C. 1400 et seq.

Jenkins, J. R., & Jenkins, L. M. (1985). Peer tutoring in elementary and secondary programs. *Focus on Exceptional Children, 17*(6), 1-12.

Jenkins, J. R., Jewell, M., Leicester, N., Jenkins, L., & Troutner, N. M. (1991). Development of a school building model for educating students with handicaps and at-risk students in general education classrooms. *Journal of Learning Disabilities, 24*, 311-320.

Johnson, S. M. (1990). *Teachers at work: Achieving success in our schools.* Scranton, PA: HarperCollins.

Joint Committee on Standards for Educational Evaluation. (1988). *The personnel standards.* Newbury Park, CA: Sage.

Joint Committee on Standards for Educational Evaluation. (1994). *The program evaluation standards.* Thousand Oaks, CA: Sage.

Joint Committee on Standards for Educational Evaluation. (in press). *The student evaluation standards.* Thousand Oaks, CA: Sage.

Joyce, B., & Calhoun, E. (1995). School renewal: An inquiry, not a formula. *Educational Leadership, 52*(7), 51-55.

Kanter, R. M. (1983). *The change masters: Innovation for productivity in the American corporation.* New York: Simon & Schuster.

Kearns, D., & Doyle, D. (1988). *Winning the brain race.* San Francisco: Jossey-Bass.

Kuhn, T. (1970). *The structure of scientific revolutions* (2nd ed.). Chicago: University of Chicago Press.

Lashley, C. (1994). Criticizing special education as a social practice. *Special Education Leadership Review, 2*(1), 40-58.

Leithwood, K., & Aitken, R. (1995). *Making schools smarter.* Thousand Oaks, CA: Corwin.

Lenz, B. K., Alley, G. R., & Schumaker, J. B. (1987). Activating the inactive learner: Advanced organizers in the secondary content classroom. *Learning Disability Quarterly, 10*, 53-56.

Lenz, B. K., Marrs, R. W., Schumaker, J. B., & Deshler, D. (1993). *The lesson organizer routine.* Lawrence, KS: Edge.

Lezotte, L. (1982). *The university role in school improvement.* Paper presented at the annual meeting of the American Education Research Association, New York.

Little, J. W. (1981). *School success and staff development in urban desegregated schools: A summary of recent completed research.* Boulder, CO: Center for Autism Research.

Little, J. W., & McLaughlin, M. (1993). *Teachers' work: Individuals, colleagues, and context.* New York: Teachers College Press.

Lortie, D. (1975). *The school teacher.* Chicago: University of Chicago Press.

MacIntyre, A. (1984). *After virtue: A study in moral theory.* Notre Dame, IN: University of Notre Dame Press.

Louis, K. S., & Kruse, S. D. (1995). *Professionalism and community: Perspectives on reforming urban schools.* Thousand Oaks, CA: Corwin.

Maheady, L., Sacca, M. K., & Harper, G. F. (1988). Classwide peer tutoring with mildly handicapped high school students. *Exceptional Children, 55*(1), 52-59.

McCarthy, M., Cambron-McCabe, N., & Thomas, S. (1998). *Public school law: Teachers' and students' rights* (4th ed.). Boston: Allyn & Bacon.

McCombs, B. L., & Whisler, J. S. (1997). *The learner-centered classroom and school: Strategies for increasing motivation and achievement.* San Franscisco: Jossey-Bass.

McLaughlin, M., & Warren, S. (1992). *Issues and options in restructuring schools and special education programs.* College Park: University of Maryland at College Park in affiliation with Westat, Inc.

Meier, D. (1995). *The power of their ideas: Lessons from a small school in Harlem.* Boston, MA: Beacon.

Morgan, G. M. (1997). *Images of organization.* Thousand Oaks, CA: Sage.

Murray, L. (1999). *Reaching for the North Star* [Videotape]. Bloomington: Indiana University, Forum on Education.

Nathan, J. (1996). Early lessons of the charter school movement. *Educational Leadership, 54*(2), 16-20.

National LEADership Network Study Group on Restructured Schools (1993). *Leadership in Education Administration Development Program.* Washington, DC: U.S. Department of Education.

Newmann, F., & Wehlage, G. (1996). *Successful school restructuring.* Madison, WI: Center on Organization and Restructuring of Schools.

New York Board of Regents. (1992). *A new compact for learning.* Albany, NY: New York State Education Department.

Olson, L. (1999). Making every test count. *Education Week, 18*(17), 11, 15-16, 18-20.

Osborne, D., & Gaebler, T. (1992). *Reinventing government: How the entrepreneurial spirit is transforming the public sector.* Reading, MA: Addison-Wesley.

Patton, M. Q. (1997). *Utilization-focused evaluation: The new century text* (3rd ed.). Thousand Oaks, CA: Sage.

Perelman, L. (1987). *Technology and the transformation of schools.* Washington, DC: National School Boards Association.

Perelman, L. (1992). *School's out: Hyperlearning, the new technology, and the end of education.* New York: William Morrow.

Peters, T. (1985). *A passion for excellence: The leadership difference.* New York: Random House.

Peters, T. (1987). *Thriving on chaos: Handbook for a management revolution.* New York: Knopf.

Peters, T., & Waterman, R. (1982). *In search of excellence: Lessons from America's best run companies.* New York: Harper & Row.

Phillips, N. B., Hamlet, C. L., Fuchs, L. S., & Fuchs, D. (1993). Combining classwide curriculum-based measurement and peer tutoring to help general educators provide adaptive education. *Learning Disabilities Research and Practice, 8*(3), 148-156.

Pomerantz, D. J., Windell, I. J., & Smith, M. A. (1994). The effects of classwide peer tutoring and accommodations on the acquisition of content area knowledge by elementary students with learning disabilities. *LD Forum, 19*(2), 28-32.

Postman, N. (1995). *The end of education: Redefining the value of school.* New York: Knopf.

Pugach, M., & Johnson, L. (1990). Fostering the continued democratization of consultation through action research. *Teacher Education and Special Education, 13*(3-4), 240-245.

Reitzug, U. C. (1998). Bureaucratic and democratic ways of organizing schools. In H. S. Shapiro & S. B. Harden (Eds.), *The institution of education.* Needham Heights, MA: Simon & Schuster.

Reynolds, M., & Birch, J. (1982). *Teaching exceptional children in all America's schools.* Reston, VA: Council for Exceptional Children.

Reynolds, M., Wang, M., & Walberg, H. (1987). *Repairing the second system for students with special needs.* Paper presented at the "Wingspread Conference on the Education of Children with Special Needs: Growing Up to Meet the Challenges of the 1990s," Racine, WI.

Riley, R. J. (1999). *State of education address.* Washington, DC: U.S. Department of Education.

Sage, D. D., & Burrello, L. (1994). *Leadership in educational reform.* Baltimore, MD: Brookes.

Sailor, W. (1991). Special education in the restructured school. *Remedial and Special Education, 12*(6), 8-22.

Sarason, S. (1982). *The culture of the school and the problem of change.* Boston: Allyn & Bacon.

Scanlon, D., Deshler, D. D., & Schumaker, J. B. (1996). Can a strategy be taught and learned in secondary-inclusive classrooms? *Learning Disabilities Research & Practice, 11,* 41-57.

Scanlon, D., Schumaker, J. B., & Deshler, D. D. (1994). Collaborative dialogues between teachers and researchers to create educational interventions: A case study. *Journal of Educational & Psychological Consultation,* 5(1), 69-76.

Scriven, M. (1991). *Evaluation thesaurus* (4th ed.). Newbury Park, CA: Sage.

Senge, P. (1990). *The fifth discipline: The art and practice of the learning organization.* New York: Doubleday/Currency.

Sergiovanni, T. (1992). *Moral leadership: Getting to the heart of school improvement.* San Francisco: Jossey-Bass.

Sergiovanni, T. (1996). *Leadership for the schoolhouse.* San Francisco, CA: Jossey-Bass.

Shadish, W. R., Jr., Newman, D. L., Sheirer, M. A., & Wye, C. (1995). *Guiding principles for evaluators* (New directions for program evaluation, No. 66). San Francisco: Jossey-Bass.

Skrtic, T. (1991). *Behind special education: A critical analysis of professional knowledge and school organization.* Denver, CO: Love.

Slaven, R. E., Madden, N. A., & Leavey, M. (1984a). Effects of cooperative learning and individualized instruction on mainstreamed, students. *Exceptional Children,* 50(5), 434-443.

Slaven, R. E., Madden, N. A., & Leavey, M. (1984b). Effects of team-assisted individualization on the mathematics achievement of academically handicapped and non-handicapped students. *Journal of Educational Psychology,* 75(5), 813-819.

Slaven, R. E., Stevens, R. J., & Madden, N. A. (1988). Accommodating student diversity in reading and writing instruction: A cooperative learning approach. *Remedial and Special Education,* 9(1), 60-66.

Spilliane, J. P. (1998). State policy and the non-monolithic nature of the local school district: Organizational and professional considerations. *American Educational Research,* 35(1), 33-63.

Spring, J. (1989). *The sorting machine revisited.* New York: Longman.

Stacey, R. D. (1996). *Complexity and creativity in organizations.* San Francisco: Berrett-Koehler.

Stainback, S., & Stainback, W. (1984). A rationale for the merger of special and regular education. *Exceptional Children,* 51(2), 102-111.

Stainback, S., Stainback, W., & Forest, M. (Eds.). (1989). *Educating all students in the mainstream of regular education.* Baltimore: Brookes.

Stainback, W., & Stainback, S. (Eds.). (1990). *Support networks for inclusive schooling: Interdependent integrated education.* Baltimore: Brookes.

Stout, J. (1988). *Ethics after Babel: The languages of morals and their discontents.* Boston: Beacon.

Thousand, J., & Villa, R. (1989). Enhancing success in heterogeneous schools. In S. Stainback, W. Stainback, & M. Forest (Eds.), *Educating all students in the mainstream of regular education.* Baltimore: Brookes.

Weick, K. (1976). Educational organizations as loosely coupled systems. *Administrative Science Quarterly, 21*(1), 1-19.

Wheatley, M. (1992). *Leadership and the new science: Learning about organization from an orderly universe.* San Francisco: Berrett-Koehler.

Wheatley, M. J. (1997). The simpler way: New metaphors for learning organizations. In L. Burrello (Producer), *America's learning* [Radio broadcast]. Bloomington: Indiana University, WFIU.

White, A., & White, L. (1992). A collaborative model for students with mild disabilities in middle schools. *Focus on Exceptional Children, 24*(9), 1-10.

Zimmerman, B. (1999). Complexity Science. *Health Forum Journal*, May-June.

Index

CORWIN
PRESS

The Corwin Press logo—a raven striding across an open book—
represents the happy union of courage and learning. We are a
professional-level publisher of books and journals for K–12 educators, and we are committed to creating and providing resources
that embody these qualities. Corwin's motto is "Success for All
Learners."

3 5282 00629 3867

Printed in the United States
70050LV00003B/273